PUDDINGS & DESSERTS

First published in Great Britain by Simon & Schuster UK Ltd, 2002
A Viacom Company

Simon & Schuster UK Ltd
Africa House
64–78 Kingsway
London
WC2B 6AH

1 3 5 7 9 10 8 6 4 2

Design and typesetting: **Fiona Andreanelli**
Food photography: **Steve Baxter**
Home economist: **Sara Buenfeld**
Stylist for food photography: **Liz Belton**
Editor: **Deborah Savage**
Printed and bound in China

ISBN 0 74322 114 1

Best-kept Secrets of the Women's Institute

PUDDINGS & DESSERTS

Sîan Cook

ACKNOWLEDGMENTS

There are so many people I would like to thank.
First of all, I would like to thank my husband, Terry,
for all his support, help and patience in helping me
with producing the manuscript on the the computer.
I would also like to acknowledge my daughters,
Holly and Amy: to thank Holly for the endless
shopping trips to shop for ingredients, for tasting
and commenting on the desserts and Amy because
she couldn't taste any of the desserts as her diet is
very restricted. I would also like to thank my friends
and neighbours for tasting and giving constructive
comments on the desserts. I have never been
so popular!

CONTENTS

INTRODUCTION

Whenever you talk about puddings and desserts with friends and family, you invariably get the **'ooh'** factor. Few people can resist a dessert, particularly if it's home-made. Many people claim not to eat puddings but, when confronted with a delicious dessert, few can resist it!

Writing this book has given me enormous pleasure. I just love desserts, particularly those including chocolate, and to be able to spend endless hours creating these recipes has been absolute heaven for me. While creating the recipes, I have been very popular with family, friends and neighbours as they have all helped by tasting the recipes and giving me their verdicts. There was one crisis while I was creating the book, which I can now look back on with amusement: I was in hospital with my younger daughter, Amy, after she had been admitted as an emergency. I had promised a friend four desserts for her party the next day. They had been prepared but not decorated so I had to give Holly (aged nine) instructions over the phone as to how to decorate them. She did a brilliant job – all those hours watching me prepare desserts had paid off!

I am lucky to be able to do what I enjoy most of all – cooking – and passing on skills and knowledge that I have acquired when I teach other people, as I do at Denman College, W.I.'s national college. My husband despairs, light-heartedly, with my obsession with anything to do with food, whether it is watching cookery programmes, reading cookery books, or studying restaurant menus and eating out. All of these are my inspiration.

I have called this book *Puddings and Desserts* as I think there is a distinction between the two. 'Puddings', such as Blackberry and Apple Crumble, conjure up an image of comfort food, often traditional, and the sort of dishes you would serve up for everyday/informal eating. On the other hand, 'desserts', such as Raspberry and Vanilla Ice Cream Gâteau, are usually a little more sophisticated, elaborate and special. It is unlikely that you would decorate a pudding but you would definitely decorate a dessert.

Desserts, as far as I am concerned, are the most important part of a meal. I plan other courses around them. When I dine out, I choose my dessert ahead of other courses! Desserts are important and should not be considered an afterthought: they are the last impression of a meal.

There is something very special about a home-made dessert. Apart from the fact that guests appreciate that time and effort have been put into preparing it, a home-made pudding is usually far superior to anything that can be bought. Supermarket desserts can look wonderful in their elaborate packaging but so often disappoint: they don't taste as good, often having a synthetic flavour, are full of additives and preservatives and invariably are very small and therefore don't look impressive when presented at the end of a meal.

I have included in this book a choice of desserts suitable for most eventualities – special and festive occasions, dinner parties, buffets and family gatherings, including healthy desserts and puddings that can be prepared quickly – and I have given some classics a makeover. Many can be prepared in advance and frozen – these are an absolute bonus as it's great to be able to either pull out a dessert from the freezer for unexpected guests or to plan a meal knowing that the dessert can be prepared well in advance and frozen.

We all lead such busy lives that it's hard to devote as much time as we would like to cooking, particularly desserts, that I nowadays make use of good-quality ready-made/convenience ingredients, where appropriate, such as custard, pastry, tarts and meringues. I know many chefs would throw their hands up in horror but, if it's a toss-up between making a pudding using these or buying one, I know which choice most people would make. You can still produce a delicious dessert but with less effort.

Generally speaking, desserts are far less elaborate nowadays than they used to be, as well as being less rich. On the other hand, presentation is often more artistic, for example, the use of height as in Fruit Stacks (page 48), making full use of different shapes such as bombes (Pashka Iced Bombe, page 54), rings (Citrus Cheese Ring, page 16) or terrines (Tiramisù Ice Cream Terrine, page 11). Their simplicity seems to enhance rather than lessen their appeal. Nowadays, decoration tends to reflect the content of the pudding, so fresh strawberries are used to decorate a Strawberry Cheesecake (page 27) and chocolate-coated coffee beans are used in Chocolate Mousse Cups (page 60), which contain both chocolate and coffee.

This book aims to demonstrate that sweet courses need not always be naughty but can be part of a healthy diet. Chapter 5 is devoted to these recipes. Other recipes can be adapted to a healthier eating plan, if low-fat ingredients are substituted for their full-fat equivalents.

When you are entertaining more than six people, it's a good idea to offer a choice of desserts. I would suggest always including a traditional dessert that guests will be familiar with, a more unusual option for those who are adventurous in their eating and a light/fruit pudding. It goes without saying that it is helpful to choose dishes that can be prepared in advance. Try to make use of seasonal ingredients, particularly fruit.

I thought it might be helpful if I included some hints and tips in this introduction that are useful for many of the recipes:

FREEZING

Each recipe tells you if it can be frozen. As a general rule, the higher the fat content of a dessert, the more likely it will freeze well. It is best to 'open freeze' and wrap the pudding in suitable packaging when frozen. To thaw, the slower the thawing process, the better the end result. I try to take desserts out of the freezer several hours before I need them and allow them to thaw gradually in the fridge. It is better to decorate a frozen dessert when it has thawed rather than before it has been frozen.

BLENDING

When ingredients are combined, they blend far better when they are of a similar consistency. That is why when folding whisked egg whites into a mixture, a recipe will usually instruct you to fold in a tablespoon of the whites to loosen the mixture before folding in the whites. It is also important to try to combine ingredients that are of a similar temperature. With melted chocolate and gelatine this is essential, otherwise you will have disastrous results.

GELATINE

Care needs to be taken when handling gelatine. Many years ago, I used to avoid any recipe that contained gelatine as I had had a few failed attempts. If you follow these instructions, you won't fail – I promise. Sprinkle the gelatine on to the liquid and not the other way round; leave the mixture to go 'spongy' for a few minutes – it will dissolve better; after melting it using any of the methods mentioned in the recipes, allow it to cool if you are adding it to a cold mixture; add a spoonful of the mixture to be set to the liquid gelatine, stir to combine and then return this to the mixture.

QUALITY

Always use the best quality and freshest ingredients that you can afford to. Doing so will pay dividends – the taste of the puddings and desserts will confirm this.

MEASUREMENTS

OVEN TEMPERATURES

Gas Mark	Electric (°C)	Fan oven (°C)
	80	60
	90	70
	100	80
E	110	90
1	120	100
1	130	110
1	140	120
2	150	130
3	160	140
3	170	150
4	180	160
5	190	170
6	200	180
6	210	190
7	220	200
8	230	210
9	240	220
9	250	230

NOTE: These temperatures are equivalent settings rather than exact conversions of degrees of heat.

VOLUME MEASURES

$1/4$ teaspoon	1.25 ml
$1/2$ teaspoon	2.5 ml
1 teaspoon	5 ml
2 teaspoons	10 ml
1 tablespoon	15 ml

NOTE: When teaspoons/tablespoons are used for measuring dry ingredients, these should be rounded (as much of the ingredient above as in the bowl of the spoon). Measuring spoons should be filled only so the top surface is level.

VOLUME MEASURES

Imperial (fluid ounces/pints)	Metric (millilitres/litres)
1 fl oz	25 ml
2 fl oz	50 ml
3 fl oz	80 ml
4 fl oz	115 ml
5 fl oz/$1/4$ pint	150 ml
6 fl oz	175 ml
7 fl oz	200 ml
8 fl oz	225 ml
9 fl oz	250 ml
10 fl oz/$1/2$ pint	300 ml
11 fl oz	325 ml
12 fl oz	350 ml
13 fl oz	375 ml
14 fl oz	400 ml
15 fl oz/$3/4$ pint	425 ml
16 fl oz	450 ml
17 fl oz	475 ml
18 fl oz	500 ml
19 fl oz	550 ml
20 fl oz/1 pint	575 ml
$1 1/4$ pints	700 ml
$1 1/2$ pints	850 ml
$1 3/4$ pints	1 litre
2 pints	1.1 litres
$2 1/4$ pints	1.3 litres
$2 1/2$ pints	1.4 litres
$2 3/4$ pints	1.6 litres
3 pints	1.7 litres
$3 1/2$ pints	2 litres

NOTE: The measurements are equivalents, not exact conversions. Always follow either the imperial or the metric measures and do not mix the two in one recipe.

WEIGHT MEASURES

Imperial (ounces/pounds)	Metric (grams/kilograms)
1 oz	25 g
2 oz	50 g
3 oz	80 g
4 oz	115 g
5 oz	150 g
6 oz	175 g
7 oz	200 g
8 oz	225 g
9 oz	250 g
10 oz	275 g
11 oz	300 g
12 oz	350 g
13 oz	375 g
14 oz	400 g
15 oz	425 g
16 oz	450 g
1 lb 1 oz	475 g
1 lb 2 oz	500 g
1 lb 3 oz	525 g
1 lb 4 oz	550 g
1 lb 5 oz	600 g
1 lb 6 oz	625 g
1 lb 7 oz	650 g
1 lb 8 oz	675 g
2 lb	900 g
3 lb	1.3 kg
3 lb 5 oz	1.5 kg

I have to admit that these are the sort of desserts I would choose from a restaurant menu – they are creamy and smooth but not too heavy after a rich meal. As they are all chilled or frozen, they have the benefit of being prepared well in advance, which I love when I am entertaining.

COOL & CREAMY

Although most of the desserts include cream, low-fat products can be substituted successfully. However, if a recipe states that it can be frozen, such as Citrus Cream Ring (page 16), don't freeze it if you have substituted a low-fat ingredient – as a general rule, the higher the fat content, the more successfully a dish will freeze.

SERVES 6–8
PREPARATION TIME:
30 minutes + 3–4 hours freezing
FREEZING: essential

Tiramisù is an extremely popular dessert and so I decided to create this variation on it. It looks impressive served as a terrine and is useful to have in the freezer for when you have unexpected guests. I like to serve it with a bowl of summer berries, such as raspberries.

TIRAMISÙ ICE CREAM TERRINE

500 g carton of custard
250 g tub of mascarpone cheese
75 ml (5 tablespoons) Marsala or
sweet sherry
50 g (2 oz) chocolate-coated coffee
beans or plain chocolate pieces
2¹/₂ tablespoons freshly ground coffee
40 g (1¹/₂ oz) caster sugar
30 ml (2 tablespoons) brandy
about 36 sponge fingers
150 ml (¹/₄ pint) double cream, whipped
cocoa powder and chocolate-coated
coffee beans, to decorate

1 Place the custard, mascarpone and Marsala or sherry in a bowl and mix thoroughly. Fold in the chocolate-coated coffee beans or chocolate pieces and set aside.
2 To make the coffee, add 250 ml (9 fl oz) of boiling water to the ground coffee in a cafetière or jug, leave to brew and then strain into a bowl. Add the sugar and brandy.
3 Line a lightly oiled 1 kg (2¹/₄ lb) loaf tin with cling film. Dip a third of the sponge fingers into the coffee mixture and place side by side in the base of the tin. Spoon half of the mascarpone mixture on top and then repeat the layers, finishing with the sponge fingers. You will probably need to fill some gaps with pieces of sponge fingers on the top layer.
4 Freeze until solid – this will probably take 3–4 hours.
5 Invert it on to a plate and decorate the top surface with the cream – if you are feeling creative, you could pipe it on top – and then finish with the beans and cocoa, sifted. Return it to the freezer and leave until the cream is frozen. Wrap it in a freezer bag and return to the freezer. Leave it in the fridge for 30 minutes to allow it to soften a little before serving.

SERVES 6–8
PREPARATION & COOKING TIME:
30 minutes + 1 hour cooking
+ 8 hours freezing
FREEZING: essential

This dessert makes an **impressive finale to a summer dinner party** or barbecue. It is actually very straightforward and can be made several days before it is needed. You could change the ice cream, sorbet and fruit to suit your preferences or what is available.

4 large egg whites
225 g (8 oz) caster sugar
700 ml (1¼ pints) vanilla ice cream, softened slightly
700 ml (1¼ pints) raspberry sorbet, softened slightly
300 ml (½ pint) double cream, whipped
fresh raspberries to decorate

1   Preheat the oven to Gas Mark 2/electric oven 150°C/fan oven 130°C. Mark three 20 cm/8-inch circles on baking parchment, cut out and place the circles on three baking sheets.
2   Place the egg whites in a large bowl and whisk on full speed until stiff but not dry. Add the sugar, a teaspoon at a time, continuing to whisk at full speed. Divide the meringue between the three circles and spread evenly with a palette knife.
3   Bake in the oven for 1 hour; the meringue is cooked when the baking parchment will easily peel away from the meringue and the bases make a hollow sound when tapped lightly, so test for this but don't peel off the paper. Turn off the oven, leave the door half open and leave the meringues in the oven until they are completely cold.
4   To assemble, peel off the baking parchment from two of the meringue circles. Place the third meringue disc in the base of a 20 cm/8-inch springform cake tin. Spoon the vanilla ice cream evenly over the meringue. Top with the second meringue disc, cover with the raspberry sorbet and top with the final meringue disc, smooth-side upwards; press down firmly. Cover and freeze for at least 8 hours.
5   To serve, remove the sides and base of the tin as well as the paper from the base. Spread the whipped cream over the surface and pile the raspberries into the centre.

RASPBERRY AND VANILLA ICE CREAM GÂTEAU

SERVES 6
PREPARATION & COOKING TIME:
30 minutes + 30 minutes cooking + 1 hour chilling
FREEZING: not recommended

PLUM & CARDAMOM FOOLS

You can enjoy this dessert throughout the year if you freeze plums when at their peak. Plums freeze very well and I discovered that their skins peel off easily on thawing. If you don't want to use any alcohol, simply replace the port with either orange juice or water.

750 g (1¾ lb) ripe Victoria plums, stoned
115 g (4 oz) caster sugar
3 cardamom pods, crushed lightly, pods discarded,
    seeds removed and crushed
45 ml (3 tablespoons) port
500 g carton of custard
150 ml (¼ pint) whipping cream, whipped, or half a 200 g
    tub of Greek-style yoghurt
1 ripe plum, stoned and cut into 6 slices, to decorate

1   Put the plums, sugar, cardamom seeds and port in a saucepan and bring to the boil. Cover and simmer very gently for at least 30 minutes until the plums are cooked and soft.
2   Strain into a bowl and allow the fruit to cool while you boil the juices for about 3–4 minutes, until they have been reduced to 45 ml (3 tablespoons).
3   Strain the juice into the plums and purée them in a food processor or blender. Fold in the custard and spoon or pour into six glass dishes. Chill for an hour.
4   Spoon or pipe the cream or yoghurt on top and decorate with a plum slice.

SERVES 4–6
PREPARATION TIME: 15 minutes + 30 minutes chilling
FREEZING: only recommended if made in freezerproof dishes

ITALIAN MOCHA FOOLS

This is simplicity itself to prepare and is an ideal finale to an Italian meal. Mascarpone and ricotta cheeses both work well in this recipe but mascarpone has far more calories.

30 ml (2 tablespoons) strong espresso coffee
30 ml (2 tablespoons) coffee liqueur,
    such as Tia Maria or Kahlua
250 g tub of mascarpone or ricotta cheese
200 g tub of Greek-style yoghurt
25 g (1 oz) demerara sugar
115 g (4 oz) amaretti biscuits, roughly crushed
amaretti biscuits, grated plain chocolate or
    chocolate-covered coffee beans, to decorate

1   Combine the coffee and alcohol. Place the chosen cheese, yoghurt and sugar in a bowl, mix well and fold in the coffee mixture.
2   Divide half the biscuits between stemmed glasses. Spoon half the mocha cream over the biscuits. Sprinkle the remaining biscuits on top, followed by the rest of the cream mixture.
3   Chill for about 30 minutes or until ready to serve.
4   Decorate with either amaretti biscuits (whole or finely crushed), grated chocolate or chocolate-covered coffee beans.

SERVES 6–8
PREPARATION TIME: 25–30 minutes + 2 hours chilling
FREEZING : recommended

CREAMY DATE & WALNUT BOMBE

This is a variation on the apricot bombe in my last book, *The WI Book of Vegetarian Cuisine*. The recipe proved to be very popular – it seems to improve on keeping and freezes very well.

225 g (8 oz) ricotta cheese
80 g (3 oz) caster sugar
80 g (3 oz) unsalted butter, melted
175 g (6 oz) dried dates, cut into small pieces
50 g (2 oz) walnuts, chopped
grated zest and juice of 3 oranges
11.7 g sachet of gelatine
8 trifle sponges, each cut horizontally into 3 slices

TO DECORATE:
150 ml (¼ pint) whipping cream, whipped
selection of seasonal fruit, prepared as necessary

1 Combine the ricotta, sugar and butter and mix well. Fold in the dates, walnuts and orange zest. Dissolve the gelatine in 30 ml (2 tablespoons) of water over a pan of hot water or by heating in the microwave for 20 seconds. Allow to cool and then add to the citrus juices in a jug.
2 Place 3–4 sponge slices in the base of a 1.1-litre (2-pint) pudding basin and spread a thinnish layer of the cheese mixture on top. Continue to layer, finishing with sponge to fit neatly on top. Strain the orange mixture and then pour very carefully over the pudding, making sure that the juices reach the bottom – this can be done by pulling back the sides with a knife. Chill for 2 hours, until set.
3 To serve, dip the basin in hot water and invert on to the serving plate. Spread the cream evenly all over the surface. Extra cream could be piped around the base. Decorate with fruit.

SERVES 6
PREPARATION TIME:
25 minutes + 15 minutes infusing + 2 hours freezing
FREEZING: essential

ORANGE MARMALADE ICE CREAM

I discovered, by accident, some time ago that syllabubs make wonderful ice cream when frozen. You could change the marmalade to suit your taste. A bitter chocolate sauce makes a perfect accompaniment.

30 ml (2 tablespoons) orange liqueur,
**   such as Cointreau or Grand Marnier**
2 tablespoons orange marmalade
1 tablespoon caster sugar
grated zest of 1 orange
300 ml (½ pint) double cream, chilled
2 egg whites, whisked stiffly
Bitter Chocolate Sauce (page 68), to serve

1 Combine the orange liqueur, marmalade, sugar and orange zest in a bowl and leave to infuse for at least 15 minutes.
2 Stir in the cream and whisk until thick.
3 Fold in a small amount of the egg whites to loosen the mixture and then gently fold in the rest of the whites.
4 Lightly oil a small (450 g/1 lb) loaf tin and line with cling film. Spoon the mixture into the tin and freeze until solid, at least 2 hours.
5 Invert on to a plate and cut into slices. Place on plates and surround with the chocolate sauce, preferably warmed.

CITRUS CHEESE RING *pictured opposite*

SERVES 6–8
PREPARATION TIME:
15 minutes + 2 hours chilling
Freezing: recommended

45 ml (3 tablespoons) water
11.7 g sachet of gelatine
395 g can of condensed milk
250 g (9 oz) curd cheese
75 ml (5 tablespoons) fresh lemon juice
15 ml (1 tablespoon) fresh lime juice
1 teaspoon finely grated lemon zest
1 teaspoon finely grated lime zest
300 ml ('/2 pint) soured cream
selection of seasonal fruit, prepared as
necessary, to serve
whipped cream and extra fruit, to
decorate (optional)

This is **a very versatile dessert** as it can be made all year round and served with whatever fruits are in season, such as fresh berries in the summer and oranges, grapes and pears in the autumn. Exotic fruit such as mangoes, papaya and physallis complement the dessert at any time.

1   Place the water in a small bowl and sprinkle the gelatine on top. Dissolve by either stirring over a pan of hot water or heating in a microwave for approximately 30 seconds on full power. Allow to cool.
2   Meanwhile, whisk all the remaining ingredients, except of course the fruit, until absolutely smooth. Beat the cooled gelatine into the cheese mixture until completely incorporated.
3   Pour it into a wetted 1.1-litre (2-pint) ring mould and place in the fridge for 2 hours to set.
4   To serve, briefly dip the mould in hot water to loosen the sides and then invert on to the serving plate. Fill the centre with your chosen fruit and, if wished, pipe cream rosettes on top of the mousse and decorate the rosettes with small pieces of fruit.

LEMON LUSH

SERVES 6
PREPARATION TIME:
15 minutes + 30 minutes chilling
FREEZING: not recommended

12 sponge fingers, broken into pieces
180 ml (12 tablespoons) fresh orange juice
300 ml ('/2 pint) double cream
juice and grated zest of 1 lemon
150 g Greek-style yoghurt
3 tablespoons good-quality lemon curd
toasted flaked almonds or
grated chocolate, to decorate

I would like to dedicate this recipe to my nieces, Katie and Annabel, as 'lush' is their favourite word. I serve it in individual glass dessert dishes but it could be served in a trifle bowl. **It would be perfect at the end of a rich or heavy meal.**

1   Divide the sponge finger pieces between the glass dishes and sprinkle 30 ml (2 tablespoons) of fresh orange juice over the sponges in each dish.
2   Pour the cream into a large bowl, add the lemon zest and juice and whisk until soft peaks form. Combine the yoghurt and lemon curd in a bowl and fold into the lemon cream. Spoon over the soaked sponges and chill until ready to serve, for at least 30 minutes if possible.
3   Just before serving, decorate with either the almonds or chocolate.

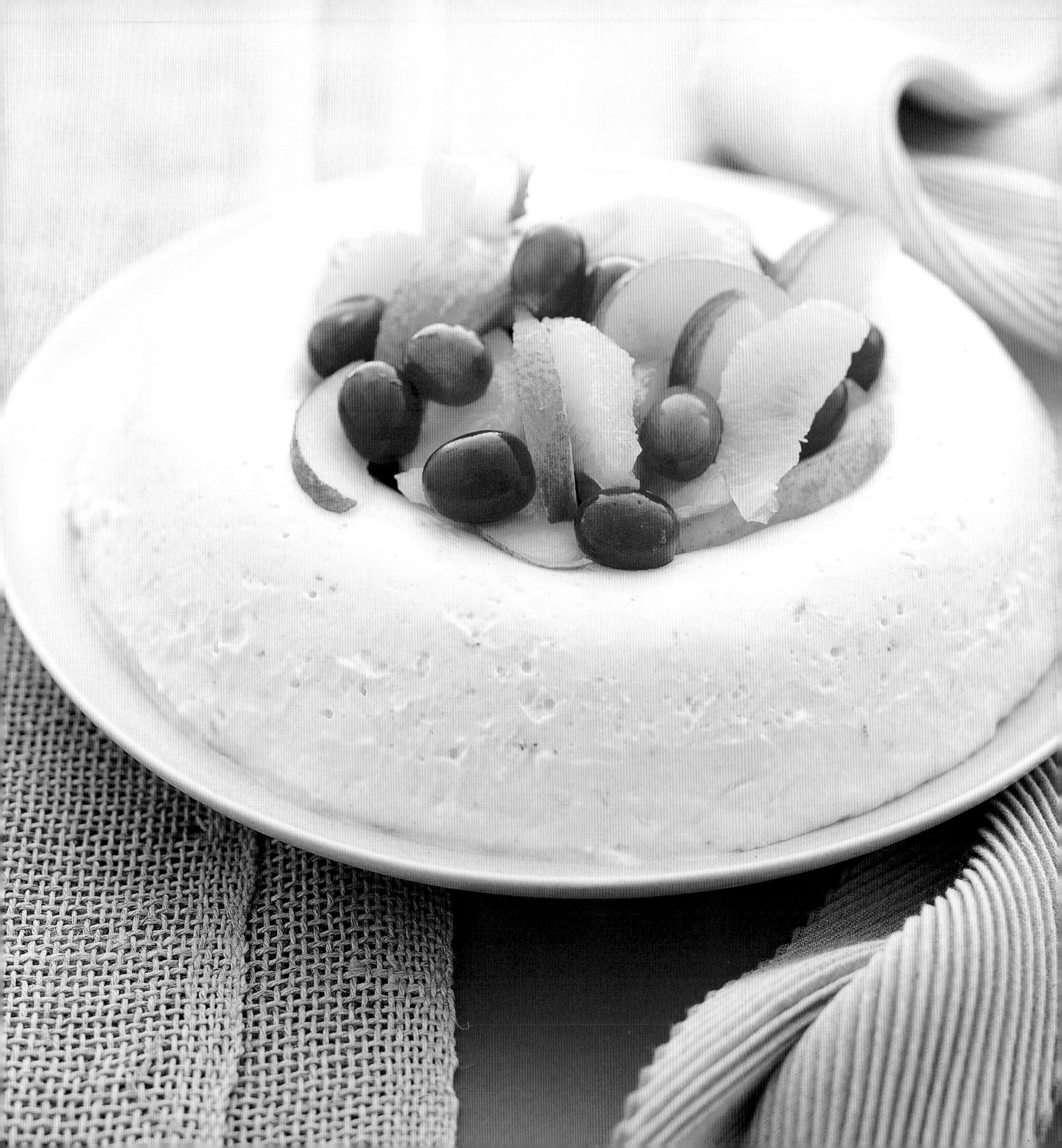

SERVES 4
PREPARATION TIME: 20 minutes + 30 minutes chilling
FREEZING: not recommended

This pretty dessert would be **ideal served at the end of a barbecue or Thai meal**. It is a good way of using up a glut of ripe peaches. You could substitute strawberries or nectarines for the peaches.

PEACH & GINGER LAYERS

5 large, ripe peaches
250 g tub of mascarpone cheese
2 pieces of stem ginger in syrup, cut into tiny pieces
30 ml (2 tablespoons) stem-ginger syrup

1 Cut two crosses at opposite ends of four of the peaches. Place them in a large bowl, pour over boiling water and leave for about 5 minutes.
2 Pour away the water and leave the peaches to cool a little.
3 Remove the skin from the peaches, cut the flesh into chunks and discard the stones. Purée the flesh.
4 Divide half the purée between four glass sundae dishes or wine glasses. Place the mascarpone in a bowl with the stem-ginger pieces and syrup and mix well. Fold in the remaining peach purée. Spoon the peach and ginger cream over the peach purée.
5 Cut the fifth peach into thin slices and use to decorate the dessert. Chill until ready to serve, for at least 30 minutes if possible.

SERVES 6–8
PREPARATION & COOKING TIME:
20 minutes + 3 hours cooking
+ chilling overnight
FREEZING: not recommended

I am enormously grateful to Julie, a friend of mine, for this recipe. It is always extremely popular. Needless to say, it is very naughty but well worth every calorie. It is lovely to make such a good dessert with only three ingredients

CARAMEL CRUNCH

395 g can of condensed milk
4 'Crunchie' bars, crumbled roughly
575 ml (1 pint) double cream

1 Place the UNOPENED can of condensed milk in a saucepan (preferably an old one) half-filled with water, bring to the boil and simmer for 3 hours, topping up the water as necessary. Refrigerate overnight.
2 Place the double cream in a large bowl and empty the contents of the condensed milk can into the cream. Whisk together until the mixture has thickened.
3 Spoon half of the caramel mixture into a glass trifle bowl, scatter half the 'Crunchies' on top and repeat the layers. Chill until ready to serve.

Many of these puddings are ones which most people have fond memories of enjoying in their childhood, with lashings of hot custard. They are extremely satisfying as well as being familiar. They are probably the most straightforward to prepare and not terribly time-consuming, apart from the time they take to bake in the oven. Most of them can be prepared partly or fully in advance and simply popped into a preheated oven when required.

FAMILY FAVOURITES

Frozen fruit can be used successfully but, as a general rule, the finished texture and appearance are usually better when fresh fruit is used, particularly in recipes made with soft fruit, which tends to be quite watery on thawing.

Different fruits can often be substituted to suit taste and availability, for example, nectarines can replace the peaches in Baked Peach and Raspberry Pudding and plums could be used instead of apples and blackberries in Blackberry and Apple Crumble (page 21).

SERVES 6
PREPARATION & COOKING TIME:
20 minutes + 25 minutes cooking
FREEZING: recommended

APRICOT & ALMOND CRUMBLE

This is a different way of making a crumble and it has the benefit of being speedy to prepare. The end result is a rather rustic one and the inclusion of the almonds in the crumble gives a lovely crunchy, nutty taste.

675 g (1 1/2 lb) fresh ripe apricots
25 g (1 oz) granulated sugar
175 g (6 oz) plain flour
80 g (3 oz) caster sugar
50 g (2 oz) blanched almonds, chopped roughly
50 g (2 oz) butter, melted

1 Preheat the oven to Gas Mark 4/electric oven 180°C/fan oven 160°C.
2 Cut the apricots in half, remove the stones and place them, cut-side down, in the bottom of a greased 1.1-litre (2-pint) buttered pie dish. Sprinkle the granulated sugar over the apricots.
3 Combine the flour, sugar and almonds in a bowl, pour in the butter and stir to form a rough crumble. Spoon evenly over the apricots and bake in the oven for 25 minutes, until the crumble is golden brown.
4 Serve warm, with custard, cream or vanilla ice cream.

SERVES 4–6
PREPARATION & COOKING TIME:
20 minutes + 40 minutes baking
FREEZING: possible

RHUBARB & GINGER SURPRISE

This is a variation on lemon surprise pudding, in which a sauce gathers underneath during cooking. Here, the orange sauce mixes with rhubarb and ginger – a lovely combination.

675 g (1 1/2 lb) young rhubarb, trimmed and cut into 2.5 cm (1-inch) pieces
80 g (3 oz) golden granulated sugar
150 ml (1/4 pint) orange juice
1–2 pieces of stem ginger in syrup, according to taste, chopped finely
25 g (1 oz) butter, softened
115 g (4 oz) soft brown sugar
2 large eggs, separated
grated zest and juice of 1 orange
25 g (1 oz) plain flour

1 Preheat the oven to Gas Mark 5/electric oven 190°C/fan oven 170°C.
2 Place the first three ingredients in a saucepan and bring to the boil; then simmer very gently until the rhubarb is soft but retains its shape.
3 Strain the rhubarb and spoon it into a greased 1.1-litre (2-pint) soufflé dish. Sprinkle the stem ginger over the rhubarb.
4 Cream the butter with half the sugar and then beat in the egg yolks, orange zest, remaining sugar and flour and finally the orange juice.
5 Whisk the egg whites until stiff, fold 1 tablespoon into the mixture to loosen it and then gently fold in the remaining whites.
6 Spoon the sponge mixture over the rhubarb and bake in the oven in a roasting tin, half filled with hot water, for 35–40 minutes, until the sponge is firm to the touch and golden brown.
7 Serve with cream or some stem-ginger ice cream.

SERVES 4–6
PREPARATION & COOKING TIME:
25 minutes + 30–40 minutes cooking
FREEZING: recommended

BLACKBERRY & APPLE CRUMBLE

Few people can resist a hot fruit crumble and blackberries and apples are always a popular combination. The crumble mixture has a nutty flavour and texture with the addition of both ground and flaked almonds.

675 g (1½ lb) Bramley apples, peeled, cored and sliced thinly
225 g (8 oz) blackberries
4 tablespoons granulated sugar
115 g (4 oz) plain flour
115 g (4 oz) ground almonds
80 g (3 oz) caster sugar
175 g (6 oz) unsalted butter
50 g (2 oz) flaked almonds

1 Preheat the oven to Gas Mark 4/electric oven 180°C/fan oven 160°C. Place the apples and blackberries at the bottom of a greased ovenproof dish and sprinkle the granulated sugar over.
2 Combine the flour, ground almonds and caster sugar in a large mixing bowl. Cut the butter into cubes and add to the bowl. Rub the butter into the flour mixture until it resembles breadcrumbs. Fold in half the flaked almonds and spoon the mixture over the fruit. Sprinkle the remaining flaked almonds on top.
3 Bake in the oven for 30–40 minutes, until the crumble is golden brown.

SERVES 4–6
PREPARATION & COOKING TIME:
15 minutes + 30 minutes cooking
FREEZING: not recommended

BAKED PEACH & RASPBERRY PUDDING

This simple but delicious pudding is delicious both hot and cold and is like a baked version of a crème brûlée. The demerara sugar on top gives a tasty contrasting texture to the creamy topping.

4 ripe peaches
150 g (5 oz) raspberries
2 large eggs
250 g tub of mascarpone cheese
225 g tub of Greek-style yoghurt
2 tablespoons demerara sugar

1 Preheat the oven to Gas Mark 5/electric oven 190°C/fan oven 170°C.
2 Halve the peaches, remove the stones and slice the flesh. Place in a large gratin dish and scatter the raspberries on top.
3 Place the eggs, mascarpone and yoghurt in a bowl and mix thoroughly with a whisk. Pour over the fruit. Sprinkle the demerara sugar on top.
4 Bake in the oven for about 30 minutes until the 'custard' has set and is golden brown.
5 Serve hot or cold with either cream or yoghurt, depending on how good you are feeling.

SERVES 6–8
PREPARATION & COOKING TIME:
30 minutes + 30 minutes chilling
+ 25 minutes cooking
FREEZING: recommended

Thin crisp tart, topped with tender pieces of rhubarb and a crunchy almond streusel, served with real vanilla ice cream or thick cream, is **an absolute winner**. My daughter, Holly, claims not to like rhubarb but her plate was clean in no time at all when she was given a slice to eat.

FOR THE PASTRY:
115 g (4 oz) butter, diced
225 g (8 oz) plain flour
80 g (3 oz) icing sugar
a pinch of salt
I large egg
a few drops of vanilla extract

FOR THE FILLING:
675 g (1½ lb) tender rhubarb, trimmed
and cut into 2.5 cm (1-inch) pieces
25 g (1 oz) stem ginger in syrup,
diced (optional)
50 g (2 oz) soft brown sugar

FOR THE STREUSEL:
50 g (2 oz) butter, diced
50 g (2 oz) ground almonds
3 tablespoons wholemeal flour
50 g (2 oz) demerara sugar

1 First, make the pastry by rubbing the butter into the flour, icing sugar and salt until the mixture resembles breadcrumbs. Make a well in the middle and add the egg and vanilla extract. Gradually work the mixture in from the edges and mix to a smooth dough. Wrap in cling film and rest in the fridge for 30 minutes.
2 Preheat the oven to Gas Mark 5/electric oven 190°C/fan oven 170°C.
3 Roll out the pastry to fit a greased 25 cm (10-inch), loose-bottomed flan tin and prick the base with a fork. Scatter the rhubarb pieces over the pastry, followed by the ginger and sugar.
4 To make the streusel topping, simply rub the butter into the ground almonds, wholemeal flour and sugar and sprinkle this over the rhubarb.
5 Bake in the oven for about 25 minutes, until both the pastry and streusel are crisp and golden brown.

RHUBARB STREUSEL TART

SERVES 6
PREPARATION & COOKING TIME:
40 minutes + 40 minutes cooking
FREEZING: recommended

GOOSEBERRY & ELDERFLOWER COBBLER

You don't often get cobblers these days, which is a shame as they are so delicious and very satisfying. They look **impressive** and would therefore be suitable for serving at a winter dinner party or Sunday lunch.

625 g (1 lb 6 oz) gooseberries, topped and tailed
115 g (4 oz) caster sugar, or to taste
a knob of unsalted butter
30–45 ml (2–3 tablespoons) elderflower cordial

FOR THE COBBLER:
225 g (8 oz) self-raising flour
a pinch of salt
100 g (3¹/₂ oz) unsalted butter, cubed
50 g (2 oz) caster sugar
1 large egg, beaten
60 ml (4 tablespoons) milk, plus extra
demerara sugar, for sprinkling

1 Place the gooseberries, sugar and butter in a saucepan and cook over a very gentle heat until the butter has melted. Add the cordial and raise the heat a little. Bring to the boil and simmer for 1 minute. Transfer to a greased ovenproof dish – approximately 27 x 17 cm (11 x 6½ inches) and 8 cm (3 inches) deep.

2 Preheat the oven to Gas Mark 6/electric oven 200°C/fan oven 180°C.

3 To make the cobbler topping, sift the flour and salt into a large bowl, add the butter and rub in until the mixture resembles breadcrumbs. Add the sugar, stir in and add the egg and two-thirds of the milk. Bring the mixture together using a knife, adding a little more milk if needed. Roll out the mixture on a floured surface to 1 cm (½ inch) thick and cut into 4 cm (1½-inch) rounds. Arrange the scones on top of the gooseberries, brush with a little milk and sprinkle with the demerara sugar. Bake for 15 minutes.

4 Reduce the temperature to Gas Mark 4/electric oven 180°C/fan oven 160°C and continue to cook for another 20–25 minutes, until the scones are cooked and golden brown.

5 Serve hot or warm, with custard or thick cream.

SERVES 6–8
PREPARATION & COOKING TIME:
25 minutes + 40 minutes cooking
FREEZING: recommended

BLACKCURRANT & ALMOND TORTE

This torte is a cross between a crumble and a shortcake. My husband was in seventh heaven after he had eaten it. You can vary the fruit according to taste and availability: raspberries and blackberries work very well indeed. If you are using frozen fruit, there is no need to thaw it beforehand.

150 g (5 oz) plain flour
1 teaspoon ground cinnamon
150 g (5 oz) caster sugar
100 g (3^1/$_2$ oz) ground almonds
50 g (2 oz) ground rice
175 g (6 oz) unsalted butter, cubed
3 medium eggs, beaten lightly
300 g (11 oz) blackcurrants, fresh or frozen
icing sugar, sifted, to decorate

1 Preheat the oven to Gas Mark 4/electric oven 180°C/fan oven 160°C.
2 Sift the flour and cinnamon together into a large bowl and then stir in the caster sugar, ground almonds and ground rice. Add the butter and rub into the flour mixture until it is like breadcrumbs. Pour in the eggs and mix together until there are no dry ingredients, being careful not to overmix.
3 Butter the base and sides of a 23 cm (9-inch) cheesecake or loose-bottomed tin and line the sides with baking parchment or greased greaseproof paper.
4 Spread just over half the mixture over the base of the tin. Sprinkle on the blackcurrants and then dot with tablespoons of the remaining mixture. Use a palette knife to spread the mixture to cover the blackcurrants (don't worry if some are still visible though).
5 Bake for 30–40 minutes, or until it is golden brown and firm to the touch. Leave to cool in the tin for 10 minutes.
6 Dust with icing sugar and serve with cream or ice cream.

SERVES 4–6
PREPARATION TIME: 25 minutes
FREEZING: not recommended

APRICOT RICE FOOL

This is basically a dessert made using storecupboard ingredients. It also is a very healthy one, with the exception of the cream, which could be replaced with yoghurt.

115 g (4 oz) ready-to-eat dried apricots
150 ml (^{1}/$_4$ pint) orange juice
575 ml (1 pint) fresh milk
25 g (1 oz) caster sugar
50 g (2 oz) ground rice
300 ml (^{1}/$_2$ pint) whipping cream, lightly whipped
toasted, flaked almonds, to decorate (optional)

1 Place the apricots and orange juice in a saucepan, bring to the boil, cover and simmer gently for 5 minutes. Allow to cool and then liquidise.
2 Place the milk and sugar in a saucepan and gradually stir in the ground rice. Bring to the boil gradually, stirring all the time and then simmer very gently for 6 minutes (or according to the pack instructions), stirring from time to time. Remove from the heat and allow to cool. Fold in a tablespoon of the apricot purée.
3 Fold the whipped cream into the rice mixture – if the rice seems quite thick, it would be an idea to fold in a tablespoon of the cream first, to loosen the mixture. Divide the remaining apricot purée between glass dessert dishes or wine glasses and then spoon the rice mixture on top. Chill until ready to serve. Decorate with toasted, flaked almonds, if wished.

These desserts are the sort you would want to serve if you want to make a big impression, whether it's for a dinner party or a buffet. They would suit a wide variety of occasions, for example, I like to serve individual desserts such as Mango and Lime Syllabubs (page 32) alongside big desserts such as Strawberry Cheesecake (page 27) on a buffet table, as people can help themselves with ease and the mixture of shapes and sizes looks attractive.

FINE & FANCY

Some of the desserts can be adapted to suit the changing seasons: make an autumn variation on Summer Fruit Roulade (page 28) by using blackberries and pears; Meringues with Raspberry Compote (page 30) can become Meringues with Clementines in Orange Jelly with Port Syllabub later in the year.

Although most of them cannot be frozen, many elements of the desserts can be prepared in advance and simply finished or assembled before serving, for example if you are making Coffee and Walnut Marshmallow Mousse with a Mocha Sauce (page 34), both the mousse and the mocha sauce can be prepared well in advance and then simply assembled before serving.

SERVES 10–12
PREPARATION TIME:
40 minutes + 3–4 hours chilling
FREEZING: not recommended

This would make a **stunning dessert** for a summer dinner party or buffet. The strawberries could be replaced with raspberries.

STRAWBERRY CHEESECAKE

FOR THE BASE:
80 g (3 oz) butter, melted
15 ml (1 tablespoon) golden syrup
225 g (8 oz) amaretti biscuits, crushed

FOR THE CHEESECAKE:
420 g can of strawberries in light syrup
11.7 g sachet of gelatine
2 x 250 g tubs of ricotta cheese
250 g tub of mascarpone cheese
50 g (2 oz) caster sugar
2 medium eggs, separated

FOR THE TOPPING:
3 tablespoons strawberry conserve
30 ml (2 tablespoons) amaretti liqueur
175 g (6 oz) fresh strawberries

1 Lightly grease a 20 cm (8-inch) cheesecake tin and make the base by combining the first three ingredients. Press them into the tin with a potato masher and chill while you make the top.

2 Drain the strawberries, reserving 150 ml (¼ pint) of the syrup. Place the syrup in a bowl, sprinkle over the gelatine and leave to soak for a minute. Stand in a bowl of hot water and stir until dissolved, or microwave on high for 1 minute and then set to one side to cool.

3 Liquidise the canned strawberries. In a large bowl, beat the strawberry purée with the cheeses, sugar and egg yolks. Add the cooled gelatine.

4 Whisk the egg whites stiffly and fold them into the strawberry mixture – it is best to fold in 1 tablespoon of the whites to loosen the mixture before adding the remainder. Spoon over the biscuit base and chill for 3–4 hours, until set.

5 Warm the conserve and liqueur together over a gentle heat and then sieve to make a clear glaze. Cut or slice the fresh strawberries and arrange on top of the cheesecake in an attractive pattern. Brush the glaze over the strawberries.

SERVES 6–8
PREPARATION & COOKING TIME:
25 minutes + 15 minutes cooking
+ 10 minutes cooling
FREEZING: recommended

Many people think that roulades are difficult to make –

they are not, as long as you follow the method carefully.

Roulades are well worth the effort because they look so

impressive. A fruit coulis, such as raspberry, would make a

perfect accompaniment to this dessert.

1   Preheat the oven to Gas Mark 5/electric oven 190°C/fan oven 170°C. Line a 30 × 23 cm (12- × 9-inch) swiss-roll tin with baking parchment or greased greaseproof paper.

2   Place the eggs and sugar in a large bowl and whisk until the mixture becomes thick and creamy and the whisk leaves a heavy trail when lifted. Sift the flour and baking powder together and then sift over the egg mixture. Fold in the flour quickly with a metal spoon, followed by the butter and the orange zest. Pour into the prepared tin and gently spread into the corners until the surface is even. Bake in the oven for about 15 minutes until the surface is golden brown and springs back when gently pressed and the sides have begun to shrink back from the sides.

FOR THE ROULADE:
4 large eggs
115 g (4 oz) caster sugar, plus extra
115 g (4 oz) plain flour
1/2 teaspoon baking powder
25 g (1 oz) butter, melted and cooled
grated zest of 1 orange

3   While the cake is cooking, cut a piece of greaseproof paper slightly larger than the tin and sprinkle generously with caster sugar. When cooked, invert the cake immediately on to the sugared paper, trim the edges and fold over one of the short edges by 2.5 cm (1 inch). Roll up the roulade, with the paper inside, and fold back the top of the paper so that it doesn't stick to the cake as it cools. Leave to cool for about 10 minutes. Unroll carefully and remove the paper.

FOR THE FILLING:
300 ml (1/2 pint) double cream, whipped
175 g (6 oz) summer fruit, such as raspberries, strawberries and redcurrants, prepared as necessary

4   Spread most of the cream over the roulade, but not right to the edges, and scatter over the fruit, reserving a few perfect berries to decorate. Roll up the filled roulade and transfer to a serving platter, preferably an oval one. Spoon the remaining cream into a piping bag and pipe rosettes on top of the roulade. Decorate with some more fruit and serve straight away.

SUMMER FRUIT ROULADE

SERVES 4
PREPARATION & COOKING TIME:
20 minutes + 20 minutes cooking
FREEZING: not recommended

ROAST PINEAPPLE WITH MANGO YOGHURT SAUCE

Roasting the pineapple gives it a delicious flavour and texture. The sauce complements it beautifully. It's hard to believe that it is so simple to prepare such a lovely dessert.

I ripe pineapple
3 tablespoons light muscovado sugar
50 g (2 oz) unsalted butter

FOR THE SAUCE:
I large, ripe mango
200 g tub of Greek-style yoghurt
25 g (I oz) caster sugar
3 drops of vanilla extract
4 small fresh mint sprigs, to decorate

I   Preheat the oven to Gas Mark 6/electric oven 200°C/fan oven 180°C.
2   Peel the pineapple and remove any 'eyes'. Cut it lengthways into four wedges and then cut each wedge into triangular slices. Arrange these slices in a single layer in a large roasting tin, sprinkle over the sugar and then dot with the butter. Roast for 20 minutes.
3   Meanwhile, make the sauce. Peel the mango, remove the stone, cut into chunks and purée. Place in a bowl and whisk with the yoghurt, sugar and vanilla extract. Spoon the sauce into a small bowl.
4   To serve, arrange the pineapple on serving plates, place a mint sprig in the centre and allow your guests to help themselves to the mango sauce.

SERVES 6
PREPARATION & COOKING TIME:
30 minutes + 1½ hours cooking + cooling
FREEZING: not recommended

MERINGUES WITH RASPBERRY COMPOTE

This is a very pretty dessert, with the white meringues sitting on a bright red sauce which complements the sweetness and crunch of the meringues beautifully. Both the meringues and the compote can be prepared in advance and simply assembled at the last minute.

2 large egg whites
115 g (4 oz) caster sugar
600 g (I lb 5 oz) fresh raspberries
about 50 g (2 oz) icing sugar
300 ml (½ pint) double cream, whipped

I   Preheat the oven to Gas Mark I/electric oven 130°C/fan oven 110°C. Line a baking sheet with baking parchment.
2   Place the egg whites in a large bowl and whisk on full speed until stiff but not dry. Add the sugar, a teaspoon at a time, continuing to whisk at full speed. Either pipe the meringue into 12 shell shapes or shape into ovals using 2 dessertspoons. Bake in the oven for 1–1½ hours, until the meringues can be lifted from the paper easily and the bases make a hollow sound when tapped lightly. Turn off the oven, leave the door half open and leave the meringues in the oven until they are completely cold.
3   To make the compote, liquidise half the raspberries with the icing sugar. Check the sweetness – you may need to add some more sugar. Pass the purée through a nylon sieve to remove the seeds. Stir in the remaining raspberries. Chill until you are ready to serve.
4   To serve, divide the compote between six serving plates. Sandwich the six pairs of meringue together with the whipped cream and place in the centre of each plate.

SERVES 6–8
PREPARATION TIME: 30 minutes + 1 hour chilling
FREEZING: recommended

APRICOT, ORANGE & ALMOND GÂTEAU

This dessert is not baked and can be prepared hours in advance. It freezes extremely well and it is worth keeping one in the freezer for when you have unexpected visitors.

80 g (3 oz) unsalted butter
80 g (3 oz) caster sugar
1 large egg yolk
115 g (4 oz) ground almonds
grated zest and juice of 2 oranges
80 ml (3 fl oz) single cream
50 g (2 oz) dried apricots, chopped finely
45 ml (3 tablespoons) Cointreau or any other orange liqueur
about 24 sponge fingers
300 ml (½ pint) whipping cream, whipped

TO DECORATE:
extra dried apricots, chopped and/or fresh orange slices
toasted flaked almonds

1 Grease a 450 g (1 lb) loaf tin and line the base and narrow sides with a strip of baking parchment or greaseproof paper.
2 Cream the butter and sugar together until light and fluffy. Add the egg yolk, almonds, orange zest and single cream and beat until smooth. Fold in the apricots.
3 Combine the orange juice and Cointreau. Dip a third of the sponge fingers, one at a time, into the orange-juice mixture and arrange in a row in the base of the tin. Spread half the almond mixture on top. Repeat the layers once more and then finish with the sponge fingers (you may need some extra orange juice). Chill in the fridge to set.
4 Turn out on to a serving dish. Spread two-thirds of the cream all over the gâteau. Pipe the remaining cream on top and decorate with the apricots/orange slices and flaked almonds.

SERVES 6–8
PREPARATION TIME: 20 minutes + 30 minutes chilling
FREEZING: not recommended

CAPPUCCINO CUPS

This is a light and elegant dessert to serve at the end of a dinner party. Ricotta cheese has a lovely creamy taste but contains about the same calories as cottage cheese.

2 medium eggs, separated
115 g (4 oz) caster sugar
2 x 250 g tubs of ricotta cheese
45 ml (3 tablespoons) very strong black coffee, cooled
30 ml (2 tablespoons) coffee liqueur,
**   such as Tia Maria or Kahlua**
chocolate-covered coffee beans
150 ml (¼ pint) whipping cream or 150 g Greek-style yoghurt
grated chocolate, to decorate

1 Place the egg yolks and sugar in a bowl and whisk until pale and creamy. Add the ricotta, coffee and half the liqueur and beat well.
2 Whisk the egg whites until they are stiff. Add a tablespoon to the ricotta mixture and beat in to loosen the mixture. Fold in the remaining whites until completely incorporated.
3 Place a few chocolate-coated coffee beans in the bottom of 6–8 (the number will depend on the size of the cups) small coffee cups. Spoon over the 'cappuccino' mixture. Whip the cream and remaining liqueur lightly or fold the liqueur into the yoghurt, if using. Spoon over the ricotta mixture to look like frothy milk. Sprinkle the grated chocolate over the 'froth'. Chill for at least 30 minutes or until ready to serve.

MANGO & LIME SYLLABUB *pictured opposite*

SERVES 4–6
PREPARATION TIME:
20 minutes + about 30 minutes chilling
FREEZING: not recommended

grated zest and juice of 2 limes
30 ml (2 tablespoons) sherry
30 ml (2 tablespoons) brandy
2 tablespoons icing sugar
2 large ripe mangoes,
peeled and stoned,
or 2 cans of mango slices, drained
230 ml (8 fl oz) double cream

Mangoes are ideal to eat after spicy food and they have a natural affinity with limes. You could vary the fruit in this syllabub to suit your tastes – you could substitute pawpaw/papaya very successfully. **I like to serve it with crisp dessert biscuits**.

1   Mix the lime zest and juice into the sherry, brandy and sugar and then set aside for a short while.
2   Put the mango flesh into a food processor and then blend to make a purée. Divide the purée between tall serving glasses and place in the fridge to chill.
3   Place the cream in a bowl and strain the brandy mixture over it, discarding the zest. Whisk it until soft peaks form (be careful not to over-whisk as the mixture will continue to thicken in the fridge). Spoon or pipe over the mango purée. Cover with cling film and return to the fridge for at least 30 minutes or until ready to serve.

NOTE: You could create a mango and lime ice cream by folding the mango purée into the syllabub mixture and freezing – there is no need to beat the mixture while it is freezing.

STRAWBERRIES ROMANOV

SERVES 4–6
PREPARATION TIME:
30 minutes + 2 hours chilling
FREEZING: not recommended

450 g (1 lb) fresh strawberries,
preferably English
30 ml (2 tablespoons) port
15 ml (1 tablespoon) Cointreau or
Grand Marnier
11.7 g sachet of gelatine
1 tablespoon icing sugar
300 ml (½ pint) whipping cream,
whipped lightly
fresh mint leaves, to decorate

This is my version of a classic dessert – it has less alcohol and uses gelatine to set the mixture a little so that the end result is less sloppy and will last a lot longer, allowing you to prepare it well in advance.

1   Wash the strawberries and remove the stalks and set aside a few perfect small ones to decorate. Cut 175 g (6 oz) of them into pieces and purée. Pass the purée through a nylon sieve. Cut the remaining strawberries into even-sized pieces and divide between glass dishes.
2   Place the port and liqueur in a bowl, sprinkle over the gelatine and leave to soak for a minute or two. Dissolve in a bowl of hot water, stirring, or place in a microwave for about 30 seconds on high. Stir well and allow to cool.
3   Meanwhile, fold the icing sugar into the strawberry purée. Whisk the gelatine into the strawberry mixture and then fold in the whipped cream. Spoon over the strawberries.
4   Chill for at least 2 hours. Just before serving, decorate with strawberries, sliced if necessary, and mint leaves.

SERVES 4–6
PREPARATION TIME:
20 minutes + 45 minutes chilling
FREEZING: not recommended

Marshmallows contain gelatine and so they act as a setting agent as well as a sweetener for this dessert. To give it an interesting dimension, pour over some mocha sauce once it has set.

COFFEE & WALNUT MARSHMALLOW MOUSSE WITH A MOCHA SAUCE

150 g (5 oz) marshmallows, halved
100 ml (3½ fl oz) hot strong black coffee
200 g tub of soft cheese
150 ml (¼ pint) double cream,
whipped to soft peaks
25 g (1 oz) walnuts, chopped

FOR THE SAUCE:
2 heaped tablespoons granulated sugar
1½ tablespoons cocoa powder
20 ml (1½ tablespoons) strong black coffee

1 Place the marshmallows and coffee in a large bowl over a pan of hot water and leave until the marshmallows have dissolved, stirring from time to time. Allow to cool a little and then place the bowl to sit in iced water until on the point of setting.

2 Fold in the soft cheese, followed by the cream and walnuts. Spoon into dessert or wine glasses and chill for 45 minutes to set.

3 To make the sauce, place the sugar and 100 ml (3½ fl oz) of water in a saucepan, bring to the boil and simmer for a minute. Add the cocoa and whisk continuously until it has been incorporated and the sauce is smooth. Remove from the heat, whisk in the coffee and allow to cool. Spread the sauce to cover the surface of the mousses completely and serve.

In the seventies and eighties, no dinner party or family meal was complete without a gâteau (especially black forest), trifle, tart, cheesecake, rice pudding or bread and butter pudding. I have taken these perennial favourites and given them a '**makeover**' to bring them into the 21st century. With the '**chifle**', I have even combined two of these popular desserts! The possibilities are endless – try experimenting yourself by taking a favourite '**oldie**' and giving it a modern image, for example, jam roly poly could become jam roly poly roulade.

RETRO PUDDINGS REVIVED

I have made use of good-quality convenience ingredients in some of the recipes – our lives are far more hectic than they were 20–30 years ago. These ingredients are trifle sponges, custard, pastry cases and lemon curd.

SERVES 10–12
PREPARATION TIME: 55 minutes + 1 hour
chilling + 30 minutes baking
FREEZING: recommended

You couldn't avoid black forest gâteau in the seventies. Made properly, it is a delicious dessert but it had a bad reputation because it was often dry and tasted synthetic. This updated version is spectacular and quite delicious – moist, very chocolatey, light and filled with kirsch-infused cherries. It is a bit time-consuming to make but well worth the effort.

1 Preheat the oven to Gas Mark 4/electric oven 180°C/fan oven 160°C. Grease a 20 cm (8-inch) cheesecake or loose-bottomed tin and base-line with baking parchment.

2 Make the sponge by whisking the sugar and eggs together in a large bowl set over a pan of hot water for about 10 minutes, until the mixture is thick and creamy. Remove from the heat and continue to whisk for a minute. Sprinkle the flour and cocoa over the surface and fold in gently, using a figure-of-eight pattern. When it is nearly all incorporated, add the melted butter and mix in. Pour the mixture into the prepared tin. Bake for 25–30 minutes, until the cake is coming away from the sides and is fairly firm to the touch.

3 Allow to cool in the tin for 5 minutes and then cool completely on a wire rack. Slice in half horizontally.

4 To make the chocolate mousse, blend the cornflour, egg yolks and half the sugar with a little of the milk until smooth. Heat the remaining milk in a small pan, pour it into the blended cornflour and stir well. Return to the pan and cook over a gentle heat until thickened, stirring constantly.

5 Remove from the heat and stir in the chocolate until it melts in the heat of the chocolate mousse. Transfer to a large bowl.

6 Meanwhile, dissolve the gelatine by sprinkling it over 3 tablespoons of water, leaving it to swell for a minute and then placing it in a bowl of hot water until it dissolves. Stir in a little of the chocolate mousse and then stir this back into the rest of the chocolate mousse. Chill until it is on the point of setting, about 15 minutes.

7 Whisk the egg whites until they are stiff and then whisk in the remaining sugar, a teaspoon at a time, until thick and glossy. Fold a tablespoon of this into the chocolate mousse to 'loosen' it and then fold in the remainder using a figure-of-eight action.

8 To assemble the gâteau, place one half of the chocolate cake in the base of the cheesecake tin (keep the other half covered until later), cut-surface upwards. Scatter two-thirds of the cherry quarters on top and sprinkle half the kirsch over the cherries. Spoon the chocolate mousse on top and then place in the fridge for about 45 minutes, to set.

9 Place the other half of the cake on top, pierce the surface lightly and sprinkle the remaining kirsch on top. Carefully loosen the sides from the cake tin and transfer to the serving plate.

10 Spread two-thirds of the cream over the surface and use the remainder to pipe rosettes around the edge. Sprinkle with the cocoa or grated chocolate and place the reserved cherry quarters on the rosettes.

FOR THE SPONGE:

4 large eggs
115 g (4 oz) caster sugar
95 g (3½ oz) plain flour, sifted
15 g (½ oz) cocoa powder, sifted
40 g (1½ oz) butter, melted

FOR THE MOUSSE:

25 g (1 oz) cornflour
3 large eggs, separated
115 g (4 oz) caster sugar
425 ml (¾ pint) milk
115 g (4 oz) plain chocolate, broken into pieces
11.7 g sachet of gelatine

FOR THE FILLING:

425 g can of black cherries in syrup, drained, stoned and cut into quarters
4 tablespoons kirsch
150 ml (¼ pint) double cream, whipped
cocoa powder or grated plain chocolate, to decorate

BLACK FOREST MOUSSE GÂTEAU

SERVES 6–8
PREPARATION TIME: 40 minutes + 2 hours chilling
FREEZING: not recommended

APRICOT & BRANDY TRIFLE

Until recently, trifles had a dated image and were not served at dinner parties. Thankfully, they have regained their popularity. I have cheated a little in this recipe by using ready-made custard – this is generally so good nowadays that there doesn't seem much point in making your own.

24 ready-to-eat dried apricots
150 ml (¼ pint) fresh orange juice
75 ml (5 tablespoons) brandy
1 packet of trifle sponges
apricot conserve
500 g carton of custard
300 ml (½ pint) whipping cream, whipped
toasted flaked almonds and dried apricots, to decorate

1   Place the apricots and orange juice in a small saucepan, bring to the boil and simmer very gently, covered, for 15–20 minutes, until very tender. Add the brandy and allow to cool.
2   Split the sponges in half, horizontally, and spread generously with the apricot conserve. Sandwich together again and cut into cubes. Put in the base of a glass trifle bowl and spoon the apricots and all the orange and brandy juices on top. Pour the custard on top and level the surface.
3   Spread two-thirds of the cream over the custard and spoon the remainder into a piping bag fitted with a star nozzle. Sprinkle the surface with the flaked almonds. Pipe cream rosettes around the edges and decorate them with dried apricot pieces. Chill for a couple of hours.

SERVES 6
PREPARATION & COOKING TIME:
15 minutes + 35–40 minutes cooking
FREEZING: not recommended

SPEEDY LEMON MERINGUE TARTS

Lemon meringue pie is quite time-consuming to make but the ready-made versions are usually disappointing. This version takes advantage of convenience foods but tastes totally home-made. You could serve the tarts with some fresh raspberries scattered around the edges of the plates.

6 ready-made sweet pastry cases
6 tablespoons good-quality lemon curd
grated zest of 2 lemons and juice of 1 lemon
2 large egg yolks
3 large egg whites
125 g (4½ oz) caster sugar

1   Preheat the oven to Gas Mark 2/electric oven 150°C/fan oven 130°C. Place the lemon curd, lemon zest, lemon juice and egg yolks in a mixing bowl and mix until all the ingredients are combined. Divide the mixture between the pastry cases, which have been placed on a baking sheet.
2   Whisk the egg whites until they are stiff and then add the sugar, a teaspoon at a time, while continuing to whisk. Spoon the mixture into a large piping bag fitted with a large star nozzle.
3   Pipe the meringue on to the lemon filling, starting with the edges and fininshing with a peak in the centre (you could simple spoon the meringue on top and 'fluff' into a peak with a palette knife).
4   Bake in the oven for 35–40 minutes, until the meringue is crisp and golden brown. Serve warm or cold.

SERVES 6
PREPARATION & COOKING TIME:
15 minutes + 30 minutes standing + 30 minutes cooking
FREEZING: not recommended

LIME BREAD & BUTTER PUDDING

This popular pudding is given a 'makeover' both in its contents and preparation. If you prefer, you can make it in a large dish rather than in individual ones.

6 slices of fruit bread
50 g (2 oz) butter, softened
lime marmalade
grated zest of 1 lime
300 ml ($^{1}/_{2}$ pint) single cream
300 ml ($^{1}/_{2}$ pint) milk
2 large eggs
2 large egg yolks
25 g (1 oz) granulated sugar

1   Butter the fruit bread slices and then spread with lime marmalade. Cut the slices into about six pieces. Butter and base-line six ramekin dishes. Layer the bread in the ramekin dishes.
2   Whisk together the lime zest, cream, milk, eggs, egg yolks and sugar and strain through a sieve into a jug. Pour the custard over the bread and leave to soak for 30 minutes.
3   Preheat the oven to Gas Mark 4/electric oven 180°C/fan oven 160°C. Bake for about 30 minutes, until the custard has set. Allow to cool a little.
4   Meanwhile, heat 1–2 tablespoons of the marmalade and sieve to remove any peel.
5   Run a knife around the edges of the puddings to loosen, invert into the palm of your hand and place in the centre of serving plates. Brush the tops with the marmalade glaze. Serve surrounded with some single cream.

SERVES 6–8
PREPARATION TIME: 30 minutes
FREEZING: not recommended

EXOTIC FRUIT TRIFLE

This variation on the traditional trifle will have your guests trying to guess the ingredients in the 'cream' topping. Including natural yoghurt in the topping makes it a lot lighter.

1 packet of trifle sponges
apricot jam
75 ml (5 tablespoons) rum or sweet sherry
2 passion fruit, halved and the pulp removed
250 g (9 oz) prepared papaya (pawpaw), cut into pieces
1 kiwi fruit, peeled and cut into wedges
155 g bar of white chocolate (Lindt is recommended), broken into pieces
300 ml ($^{1}/_{2}$ pint) whipping cream, whipped to soft peaks
500 g (1 lb 2 oz) natural yoghurt
1 large ripe mango, peeled and the flesh puréed

TO DECORATE:
slices of fresh mango and kiwi fruit
grated plain chocolate

1   Cut the trifle sponges in half horizontally, spread with jam, sandwich together and cut into cubes. Place in the base of a glass bowl and sprinkle the rum or sherry over the sponges.
2   Scatter the passion fruit pulp over the sponges, followed by the papaya and kiwi fruit.
3   Melt the chocolate in a bowl over a pan of barely simmering water. Allow to cool. Combine half the cream with the yoghurt and the mango purée. Fold in the melted white chocolate.
4   Spoon the white chocolate cream over the trifle base. Spread or pipe the remaining cream on top and decorate with the mango, kiwi fruit and grated plain chocolate. Chill for at least 2 hours or until ready to serve.

SERVES 6
PREPARATION & COOKING TIME:
20 minutes + 20 minutes cooking
FREEZING: not recommended

THAI RICE PUDDING BRÛLÉES

I am not a rice pudding fan but I love this version, which uses rice flakes to give a creamier texture and lime, coconut and cardamom to give a subtle Thai flavour. Brûlées are very popular at the moment and so I decided to add a brûlée topping to give it an up-to-date dimension.

50 g (2 oz) flaked pudding rice
50 g (2 oz) caster sugar
I lime
3 cardamom pods, crushed open
300 ml ($^1/_2$ pint) semi-skimmed milk
300 ml ($^1/_2$ pint) coconut milk
300 ml ($^1/_2$ pint) double cream, whipped to soft peaks
demerara sugar

I Place the rice in a saucepan with the sugar, a few pieces of the lime zest, cardamoms, and both milks. Bring to the boil over a moderate heat, stirring from time to time. Simmer over a low heat for about 15–20 minutes, stirring every now and then to prevent it from sticking, until the rice is cooked and the milk has been absorbed.

2 Allow to cool and then remove the lime zest and the cardamoms.

3 Fold in the cream, followed by the juice of the lime, and spoon into six ramekin dishes. Sprinkle demerara sugar generously over the surfaces of the puddings and place under a hot grill until the sugar has caramelised.

4 Chill for at least an hour or until ready to serve.

SERVES 4–6
PREPARATION TIME: 20 minutes + 4 hours freezing
FREEZING: essential

BROWN BREAD ICE CREAM

I first heard of this ice cream in the early eighties and thought it very strange but, on tasting it in a restaurant, became hooked. It can either be served with a fruit coulis such as raspberry or, if you are feeling indulgent, a butterscotch or toffee sauce.

115 g (4 oz) wholemeal breadcrumbs
50 g (2 oz) demerara sugar
425 ml ($^3/_4$ pint) double cream
30 ml (2 tablespoons) brandy
50 g (2 oz) icing sugar, sifted

I Preheat the oven to Gas Mark 6/electric oven 200°C/fan oven 180°C.

2 Arrange the breadcrumbs evenly on a baking sheet and bake for about 10 minutes or until the crumbs are golden, stirring occasionally. Allow to cool and then break down any lumps into crumbs.

3 Whisk the cream, brandy and icing sugar together until thickened and then pour into a shallow container. Freeze for $1^1/_2$–2 hours, or until the mixture is mushy.

4 Transfer to a bowl and whisk to a smooth consistency. Stir in the breadcrumbs, return to the shallow container, cover and freeze until firm, another $1^1/_2$–2 hours or so.

5 To serve, transfer to the fridge half an hour before eating, so that it softens up a little gradually.

SERVES 8
PREPARATION TIME: 40 minutes + 2 hours chilling
FREEZING: recommended

CHOCOLATE & AMARETTI CRUNCH CHEESECAKE

I once made an ice cream with these ingredients and then decided to turn it into a modern-day cheesecake. The pieces of chocolate and amaretti biscuits provide an **interesting contrast** to the creaminess of the rest of the filling. I have used ricotta cheese to create a lighter taste but you could use a cream or curd cheese instead.

175 g (6 oz) digestive biscuits, crushed
50 g (2 oz) butter, melted

FOR THE FILLING:
11.7 g sachet of gelatine
2 x 250 g tubs of ricotta cheese
115 g (4 oz) caster sugar
100 g (3^1/$_2$ oz) plain chocolate, cut into small pieces
100 g (3^1/$_2$ oz) amaretti biscuits, crushed roughly
350 ml (12 fl oz) double cream, whipped to soft peaks
cocoa powder, to decorate

1 Lightly oil a 20 cm (8-inch) cheesecake or springform tin. Combine the digestive biscuits and butter, spoon into the tin and press down with a potato masher. Chill while you make the filling.
2 Measure 3 tablespoons of water into a small bowl, sprinkle over the gelatine and leave to go 'spongy' for a minute or two. Dissolve by placing the bowl in a larger bowl of hot water and stirring. Alternatively, you could microwave it on high for 30 seconds. Allow to cool.
3 Combine the ricotta and sugar in a large bowl and mix well. Beat in the cooled gelatine and then fold in the chocolate and amaretti biscuits, followed by the cream. Spoon on to the biscuit base and chill for a couple of hours, or until set.
4 Run a knife around the sides of the cheesecake and remove the sides of the tin. Sift cocoa powder on top to decorate and serve.

SERVES 8
PREPARATION TIME:
30 minutes + 1 hour chilling
FREEZING: not recommended

I have called this dessert a '**chifle**' because it is a cross between a cheesecake and a trifle and I have to say it is a winning combination. Raspberries and white chocolate go so well together but you could alter the fruit to suit your taste and what is available. Care needs to be taken when melting the chocolate as white chocolate is not as stable as dark.

4 trifle sponges
45 ml (3 tablespoons) brandy or kirsch
225 g (8 oz) fresh or frozen and thawed raspberries
500 g carton of custard
250 g cream cheese
50 g (2 oz) caster sugar
110 g (4 oz) white chocolate, melted and cooled
300 ml (½ pint) whipping cream, whipped
fresh raspberries and mint leaves, to decorate

1   Cut the sponges into small pieces and place in the bottom of a glass serving bowl. Sprinkle the brandy or kirsch over. Spoon the raspberries over the sponges.
2   Divide the custard between two large bowls. Add the cream cheese and half the sugar to one and mix thoroughly. Add the chocolate and remaining sugar to the other and mix well. Add half the cream to the chocolate mixture and fold in thoroughly.
3   Spoon the cream cheese mixture on to the raspberries, levelling the surface, and then repeat with the chocolate mixture. Spread the remaining cream on top. Pile some fresh raspberries in the middle and chill for at least 1 hour or until ready to serve. Decorate with fresh mint.

RASPBERRY & WHITE CHOCOLATE 'CHIFLE'

The idea of healthy puddings seems to be a contradiction in terms. While no one can deny that rich, calorie-laden desserts are an absolute joy, healthy desserts can also be very enjoyable. As a nation, we are being encouraged to eat a healthier diet by lowering the fat, cholesterol, salt and sugar in our diet, increasing the fibre and eating at least five pieces of fruit and vegetables each day. By following these guidelines, you can still enjoy interesting and tasty desserts by including a wide variety of fresh and dried fruits and substituting a low-fat product for the full-fat version, for example, ricotta cheese for cream cheese, Elmlea for fresh cream, Greek-style or ordinary yoghurt for cream, half-fat/reduced-fat custards for the richer kind and so forth.

HEALTHY PUDDINGS

Quite often, you don't have room for a rich dessert at the end of a meal but could manage something light. These desserts would fit the bill perfectly. In fact, if you are offering a choice of desserts, I would always recommend including a dessert such as one of these.

SERVES 4
PREPARATION & COOKING TIME: 15 minutes
FREEZING: not recommended

This is such a versatile and speedy dessert. It can be served simply as it is, in which case it is light and not too calorific, or it can be served with some good-quality vanilla ice cream. If you want to go completely over the top, as I did when I prepared it for my husband, serve it with chocolate fudge cake and cream for a variation on black forest gâteau!

PLUM, CHERRY & PORT COMPOTE

2 tablespoons plum jam
80 g (3 oz) caster sugar
450 g (1 lb) Victoria plums, quartered and stoned
225 g (8 oz) cherries, stoned if you wish
115 ml (4 fl oz) port, preferably ruby
grated zest of 1 orange

1   Put the jam and sugar in a large shallow pan and heat gently until the jam melts, stirring from time to time.
2   Add the plums and cherries and continue to cook over a gentle heat, stirring carefully so that you don't break up the plums, until the fruit juices begin to be released into the jam juices.
3   Add the port and orange zest, bring to the boil, reduce the heat immediately and simmer for a couple of minutes until the fruit is cooked.
4   Serve immediately or allow to cool and chill.

SERVES 4
PREPARATION & COOKING TIME:
15 minutes + 15 minutes cooking
FREEZING: not recommended

You can vary the fruit according to your preferences and what's in season. In the summer, place the parcels on the barbecue to cook while you eat your main course. The alcohol can be replaced by fruit juice, such as more orange or pineapple.

BAKED FRUIT PARCELS

about 900 g (2 lb) prepared weight of fruit,
        e.g. strawberries, pineapple, peaches and
        grapes, sliced, peeled or cut as appropriate
clear honey, to taste
60 ml (4 tablespoons) fresh orange juice
60 ml (4 tablespoons) liqueur, such as rum or Cointreau

1   Preheat the oven to Gas Mark 6/electric oven 200°C/fan oven 180°C.
2   Cut four large squares of foil (or one very big square). Divide the fruit between the foil in a single layer. Drizzle over the honey, fruit juice and liqueur. Scrunch the foil to seal completely, place on a baking sheet and bake in the oven for 12–15 minutes.
3   Transfer to serving plates and allow your guests to open their own parcels. Serve with some thick cream or vanilla ice cream.

SERVES 6
PREPARATION TIME:
25 minutes + 1–2 hours chilling
FREEZING: not recommended

This dessert tastes as if it is laden with calories but it has surprisingly few (only 162 per dessert), because it uses low-fat ricotta instead of cream cheese. It is very **refreshing and light** and therefore ideal to serve after a rich or heavy meal.

CREAMY MOUSSES WITH PASSION FRUIT & PAPAYA COULIS

115 ml (4 fl oz) fresh orange juice
37 ml (2¹/₂ tablespoons) fresh lemon juice
11.7 g sachet of gelatine
450 g (1 lb) ricotta cheese
grated zest from 1 orange and 1 lemon
3 large egg whites, whisked stiffly

FOR THE COULIS:
4 passion fruit
1¹/₂ ripe papayas (pawpaws)
175 ml (6 fl oz) fresh orange juice
6 physalis, to decorate

1 Pour the orange and lemon juices into a cup or small bowl, sprinkle the gelatine on top and leave until it becomes sponge-like. Dissolve by placing the cup/bowl in a pan of hot water and stirring or microwave on high for 30–40 seconds. Allow to cool.

2 Meanwhile, place the ricotta cheese and citrus zests in a bowl and beat to mix thoroughly. Stir in the cooled citrus juices. Fold in a tablespoon of the egg whites to loosen the mixture and then fold in the remaining egg whites gently, until they have been thoroughly incorporated. Spoon into six base-lined ramekins and chill for 1–2 hours, until set.

3 Cut the passion fruit in half and scoop the flesh with a teaspoon into a sieve placed over a bowl. Press the flesh to extract as much juice as possible. Place the juice, with the flesh from the papaya and the orange juice, in a liquidiser or blender and blend until smooth.

4 Unmould a mousse on to the centre of each serving plate and surround with the coulis. Unwrap the papery skin from each physalis, twist and place one in the centre of each mousse.

SERVES 4–6
PREPARATION TIME: 15 minutes
FREEZING: not recommended

This refreshing dessert has the benefit of being both **healthy and quick** to prepare. It would be an easy way of ensuring that the family get their daily vitamin C quota as kiwis are packed with this vitamin. It could also be served in tall wine glasses at the end of a rich or heavy meal. The kiwis can be sieved or the pips left: I think that the black pips look quite attractive. The fools are best eaten soon after they are made.

KIWI FOOLS

4 kiwi fruit, peeled
500 g tub of low-fat custard
250 g tub of ricotta cheese
extra sugar to taste (optional)

1   Peel the kiwi fruit and cut one in half. Set one half aside for decorating and purée the flesh of all the remaining fruit.
2   Place the custard and ricotta cheese in a bowl and mix thoroughly. Fold in the kiwi-fruit purée. Add a little extra caster sugar if the fool isn't as sweet as you would like.
3   Spoon the fool into tall wine glasses. Cut the remaining kiwi fruit into thin slices and each slice into quarters. Arrange these pieces attractively on top of the fools. Chill until ready to serve.

SERVES 4–6
PREPARATION TIME: 20 minutes
FREEZING: not recommended

This is such a refreshing fruit salad. I served it after a barbecue on one of those rare, hot, balmy summer evenings and it was ideal. A good accompaniment would be a sorbet, such as lemon.

GREEN FRUIT SALAD

75 ml (5 tablespoons) lime cordial
150 ml ($^1/_4$ pint) water
50 g (2 oz) caster sugar
grated zest and juice of 1 lime
115 g (4 oz) white seedless grapes,
      halved
3 kiwi fruit, peeled and sliced
1 large Granny Smith apple, quartered,
      cored and sliced
1 Ogen melon, peeled, de-seeded and cut
into chunks

1   Combine the lime cordial, water, sugar and lime zest and juice in a jug and stir until the sugar has dissolved.
2   Arrange the fruit in a large glass serving bowl and pour over the lime syrup. Chill until ready to serve.

FRUIT STACKS *pictured opposite*

SERVES 6
PREPARATION & COOKING TIME:
30 minutes + 10 minutes cooking
FREEZING: not recommended

**fruit of your choice, such as peaches,
bananas, strawberries and
raspberries, prepared as necessary
6 sheets of filo pastry
25 g (1 oz) butter, melted
200 g tub of low-fat/light soft cheese
150 g tub of Greek-style yoghurt
2 tablespoons runny honey
icing sugar, sifted, to decorate**

'Stacks' are very much in **vogue** with trendy restaurants. These are incredibly easy to make as well as being very light and healthy.

1 Preheat the oven to Gas Mark 6/electric oven 200°C/fan oven 180°C.
2 Lightly brush the surface of a baking sheet with a little of the butter. Brush the filo sheets with the remaining butter and cut out circles using a 9 cm (3½-inch) pastry cutter (you could use a small saucer if you don't have a suitable cutter). Place on the baking sheet and bake in the oven for about 10 minutes, until crisp and golden. Cool on a wire rack.
3 Place the soft cheese, yoghurt and honey in a bowl and mix together. Cut any large fruit into even-sized pieces.
4 To assemble, place pastry circles on six serving plates, spoon a spoonful of the creamy mixture in the centre, top with some fruit and repeat the layers, finishing with the pastry. Dust with some icing sugar and serve.

BLACKBERRY MOUSSES

SERVES 6
PREPARATION TIME: 20 minutes
FREEZING: not recommended

**350 g (12 oz) fresh or frozen blackberries
80 g (3 oz) caster sugar
11.7 g sachet of gelatine
250 g tub of ricotta cheese
200 g tub of light cream cheese
2 large egg whites, whisked to stiff peaks
fresh mint leaves, to decorate**

It's hard to believe that this deliciously creamy dessert is so healthy – **low in fat and calories**, high in vitamin C! The blackberries could be replaced by raspberries or strawberries, if wished.

1 Place the blackberries (reserving a few to decorate), caster sugar and 30 ml (2 tablespoons) of water in a saucepan and bring to the boil over a moderate heat. Lower the heat straight away and simmer very gently for 3–4 minutes.
2 Sieve the blackberries and their liquid into a bowl to remove the pips and then sprinkle the gelatine over the purée. Whisk with a hand whisk or stir with a spoon until the gelatine has dissolved. Allow to cool.
3 Beat the ricotta and cream cheeses together in a bowl and stir in the blackberry mixture. Fold in a tablespoon of the egg whites with a metal spoon to loosen the mixture and then fold in the remaining whites until there is no white visible.
4 Spoon into wine glasses or glass dessert dishes and decorate with the reserved blackberries and mint leaves.

This recipe conjures up images of the Caribbean, with all its lovely tropical fruit flavours. It's nice to prepare a dessert that is healthy and yet so utterly delicious. You could drizzle a little rum over the fruit to give it an alcoholic '**kick**'. This sorbet is very quick to prepare using the food processor: don't despair if you don't have one – you could use a hand blender.

SERVES 6–8
PREPARATION TIME:
25 minutes + 3 hours freezing
FREEZING: essential

MANGO & GINGER SORBET WITH TROPICAL FRUIT

3 large, ripe mangoes, peeled, stoned and cut into 2.5 cm (1-inch) chunks
juice of 1 lime
1 piece of stem ginger in syrup, chopped
150 ml (¼ pint) fresh orange juice
150 g (5 oz) caster sugar
1 papaya (pawpaw)
1 small pineapple
2 kiwi fruit
1 large banana

1 To prepare the sorbet, place two of the mangoes, the lime juice, stem ginger, orange juice and caster sugar in a food processor and purée them. Transfer the purée to a non-reactive metal bowl and freeze for 2 hours (the centre may still be a bit soft).

2 Spoon the sorbet back into the food processor and process until smooth, being very careful not to over-process or it will melt. Pour it into a plastic carton and freeze until solid – about another hour.

3 Prepare the fruit: peel and de-seed the papaya and cut into 2.5 cm (1-inch) chunks; peel the pineapple and cut into the same sized chunks; peel the kiwi fruit and cut each into six wedges; finally, peel the banana and cut into large chunks. Scoop the sorbet on to dessert plates and arrange the prepared fruit attractively around the sorbet.

NOTE: The sorbet will keep for several days in the freezer but you will need to reprocess it and re-freeze it for 15 minutes to make sure there are no ice crystals.

While it is by no means essential to serve a dessert that is appropriate to a festive occasion, I think it makes that occasion special if you do, even if you do what so many restaurants do, for example on Valentine's Day, by giving their usual desserts a romantic name and/or shaping them as hearts.

On the subject of shape, if you are not a fan of cranberries, you could still create a Christmas dessert by filling the Pear and Cranberry Crackers (page 56) with your favourite fruit or mincemeat instead.

FESTIVE DESSERTS

Some of these desserts can be adapted to suit another festive occasion, for example, Festive Pavlova (page 52) could be shaped into a heart and filled with cream and fruit, Toffee Apple Baked Alaska (page 57) could be filled with clementines and mincemeat ice cream (you can buy this or make your own by folding mincemeat into softened vanilla ice cream) for a New Year's Eve celebration.

SERVES 6–8
PREPARATION & COOKING TIME:
30 minutes + 1 hour cooking
+ 1 hour cooling
FREEZING: recommended

I am not a lover of Christmas pudding and so I am always on the lookout for good alternatives. I adore chocolate and meringue so this is a **winner** as far as I am concerned.

FESTIVE PAVLOVA

FOR THE MERINGUE:
225 g (8 oz) icing sugar
1 tablespoon cocoa powder
2 teaspoons cornflour
4 large egg whites
a pinch of salt
1 teaspoon white-wine vinegar

FOR THE TOPPING:
115 g (4 oz) plain chocolate (at least 70% cocoa solids)
250 g can of sweetened chestnut purée
30 ml (2 tablespoons) dark rum or brandy
250 ml (9 fl oz) double cream, whipped to soft peaks

1 Preheat the oven to Gas Mark 1/electric oven 130°C/fan oven 110°C. Place a piece of baking parchment on a baking sheet and mark a 20 cm (8-inch) circle on it.

2 Sift 3 tablespoons of icing sugar with the cocoa and cornflour. Whisk the egg whites in a large bowl until they are frothy. Add the salt and continue to whisk until they are stiff. Continue to whisk, adding a teaspoon of icing sugar at a time, making sure each teaspoon has been incorporated before adding the next. Fold in the sugar and cocoa mixture and then quickly fold in the vinegar.

3 Spoon or pipe the meringue on to the parchment circle and make the sides higher than the centre. Bake in the oven for an hour until it is set.

4 Turn off the oven and leave the pavlova in the oven until it has cooled – at least an hour. At this stage the pavlova will crack – don't worry about this.

5 Melt 80 g (3 oz) of the chocolate in a bowl set over a pan of hot water (or you could melt it in the microwave). Put the chestnut purée in a bowl together with the rum or brandy and beat until it is smooth. Add the melted chocolate and mix thoroughly. Fold in half the cream and spoon on to the pavlova. Spoon the remaining cream on top and grate the remaining chocolate on top of the cream. Serve with single cream.

I just love this dessert. The texture of the mousse and the combination of white chocolate with passion fruit creates a really special dessert which is a perfect end to a romantic meal such as on Valentine's Day. If you have any heart-shaped moulds, you could prepare the mousses in them.

SERVES 6
PREPARATION TIME:
20 minutes + 2 hours chilling
FREEZING: recommended

WHITE CHOCOLATE & PASSION FRUIT MOUSSES

2 teaspoons gelatine
200 g tub of cream cheese
200 g tub of Greek-style yoghurt
300 g (11 oz) good-quality white chocolate, such as Lindt, melted and cooled
2 large eggs, separated
3 large passion fruit
a few pieces of exotic fruit, such as mango, kiwi fruit and papaya (pawpaw), prepared and diced, to decorate

1 Lightly oil six ramekin dishes and base-line with discs of baking parchment.
2 Measure 3 tablespoons of cold water into a small bowl and sprinkle over the gelatine. Leave to go 'spongy' for a minute or two and then dissolve by placing the bowl in a larger one containing hot water, stirring. Alternatively, place the bowl in the microwave and cook on high for 20 seconds. Allow to cool.
3 Place the cream cheese and yoghurt in a large bowl and beat together. Beat in the white chocolate until it is thoroughly incorporated, then the egg yolks, followed by the gelatine.
4 Halve two of the passion fruit, scoop out the pulp and seeds and stir into the mixture (you can omit the seeds, if wished).
5 Whisk the egg whites stiffly. Fold a tablespoon into the mixture to lighten it and then fold in the rest. Spoon the mousse into the ramekin dishes. Chill until set.
6 Run a knife around the edge of each dish and invert on to the serving plates. Remove the pulp and seeds from the remaining passion fruit and put some on top of each mousse. Decorate each mousse with the diced exotic fruit.

CLEMENTINES IN ORANGE JELLY WITH A PORT SYLLABUB

pictured opposite

SERVES 6
PREPARATION TIME:
20 minutes + 30 minutes chilling
FREEZING: not recommended

4 clementines, peeled
I packet of orange jelly
150 ml (¹/₄ pint) freshly squeezed
orange juice

FOR THE PORT SYLLABUB:
150 ml (¹/₄ pint) ruby port
juice of I lemon
65 g (2¹/₂ oz) caster sugar
225 ml (8 fl oz) double cream

This pretty dessert includes festive ingredients but in a much lighter style than many traditional Christmas desserts. The syllabub complements the clementine jelly beautifully.

1 Segment the clementines and cut each segment in half. Divide the clementines between six glass sundae dishes or wine glasses.
2 Make up the jelly with 300 ml (¹/₂ pint) of boiling water and, once it has dissolved, add the orange juice. Pour the jelly over the clementines and chill for 30 minutes or longer, until the jelly has set.
3 Place the port, lemon juice and sugar in a large bowl and stir until the sugar has dissolved. Stir in the cream and whisk until the cream is just beginning to hold its shape. Pour over the jellies and refrigerate until ready to serve.

PASHKA ICED BOMBE

SERVES 6
PREPARATION TIME:
40 minutes + 3 hours freezing
FREEZING: essential

50 g (2 oz) sultanas
25 g (I oz) dried apricots, chopped into
small pieces
45 ml (3 tablespoons) amaretto liqueur
125 g (4¹/₂ oz) marzipan, cut into
small pieces
500 g tub of custard
200 g tub of cream cheese
150 ml (¹/₄ pint) double cream, whipped

FOR THE CHOCOLATE BALLS:
125 g (4¹/₂ oz) marzipan
80 g (3 oz) plain chocolate, melted

Pashka is a Russian dessert traditionally served at Easter. This iced version has some of the ingredients usually included in the dessert but I have added marzipan, which is in simnel cake, and amaretto liqueur to complement the almond in the marzipan. The chocolate marzipan balls represent the disciples, again as on a simnel cake.

1 Soak the sultanas and the apricots in the amaretto for 20–30 minutes.
2 In the meantime, place the marzipan and custard in a saucepan and heat over a moderate heat, stirring, until the marzipan melts. Allow to cool a little.
3 Whisk the cream cheese into the custard mixture and fold in the soaked dried fruit, with its soaking liquid, followed by the cream.
4 Lightly oil a 1-litre (1³/₄-pint) pudding basin and line with cling film. Spoon the pashka into the basin and freeze until solid, about 3 hours.
5 To make the chocolate marzipan balls, divide the marzipan into 12 or 13 pieces and roll into balls. Using two teaspoons, dip the balls into the melted chocolate and place on a piece of baking parchment to set.
6 To serve, invert the bombe on to the serving dish, peel off the cling film and surround with the chocolate balls.

SERVES 6
PREPARATION & COOKING TIME:
30 minutes + 30 minutes cooking
FREEZING: not recommended

PEAR & CRANBERRY CRACKERS

These filo pastry crackers make a novel alternative to Christmas pudding. They can be made in advance and then simply popped into the oven to warm through. **I like to serve them with a brandy custard** – just add a good splash of brandy to custard and stir in. It is worth noting that you should keep the remaining filo pastry sheets covered while you are making the crackers, otherwise they will dry out.

18 small sheets filo pastry (I used **Cypressa's**, from **Waitrose**)
80 g (3 oz) butter, melted
caster sugar

FOR THE FILLING:
grated zest and juice of I lemon
50 g (2 oz) caster sugar, plus extra for sprinkling
2 tablespoons ground almonds
I teaspoon ground cinnamon
4 large pears, peeled, cored and diced
115 g (4 oz) fresh cranberries
50 g (2 oz) chopped walnuts

1 Preheat the oven to Gas Mark 5/electric oven 190°C/fan oven 170°C.
2 Combine the filling ingredients in a large bowl and mix thoroughly.
3 Lay one sheet of pastry on the work surface, brush with the melted butter and repeat with two more sheets. Spoon a sixth of the pear and cranberry mixture on to the long side nearest to you, leaving a gap at either end.
4 Roll up the pastry to enclose the filling – you should end up with the seam underneath. Pinch each end to create a cracker. Brush with the melted butter and lay on a baking sheet. Repeat to make six crackers.
5 Sprinkle each cracker with caster sugar and bake in the oven for about half an hour. Check them after 10–15 minutes; you will probably need to cover the 'ends' with pieces of foil to prevent them from burning before the centres of the crackers are cooked.
6 Serve hot or warm, with brandy custard.

SERVES 6–8
PREPARATION & COOKING TIME: 20 minutes
FREEZING: not recommended

TOFFEE APPLE BAKED ALASKA

A baked alaska is an ideal dessert to serve on bonfire night, particularly if you present it at the table with lit sparklers pressed into the meringue. The filling includes toffee ice cream and apple chunks, in keeping with the toffee apples traditionally associated with this night. This is a very speedy dessert to prepare as the only part of it that requires any preparation is the meringue.

25 cm (10-inch) sponge flan case
350 g jar of chunky apple pieces
500 ml tub of toffee (or fudge) ice cream
4 large egg whites
225 g (8 oz) caster sugar
icing sugar and sparklers, to serve

1   Preheat the oven to Gas Mark 8/electric oven 230°C/fan oven 210°C.
2   Place the sponge on an ovenproof serving dish. Spread the apple pieces over the surface, avoiding the raised edges, and then spread the ice cream over the apples. Place in the freezer while you make the meringue.
3   Place the egg whites in a large bowl and whisk on a fast setting until stiff but not dry. Add the sugar, a teaspoon at a time, while continuing to whisk at high speed, until the meringue is thick and glossy.
4   Remove the dish from the freezer and spread the meringue all over the ice cream and sponge, making sure that there are no gaps in the meringue.
5   Place in the oven straight away and bake for 3–4 minutes, until the meringue is golden brown. Dust with icing sugar, place lit sparklers in the meringue and serve immediately.

SERVES 8–10
PREPARATION & COOKING TIME: 30 minutes + chilling overnight
FREEZING: recommended

CHOCOLATE LOG

This log will look very impressive served after a Christmas meal and the fact that it freezes so well means that you can prepare it well in advance. It is quite rich so it is best to serve in small slices with some brandy sauce or a fruit compote.

115 g (4 oz) dried berries and cherries (or dried cranberries)
45 ml (3 tablespoons) brandy or kirsch
200 g (7 oz) cream cheese
175 g (6 oz) plain chocolate (at least 70% cocoa solids), melted
300 ml ($\frac{1}{2}$ pint) double cream, whipped
16 digestive biscuits
icing sugar and Christmas decorations, to decorate

1   Place the dried berries and cherries and brandy or kirsch in a food processor and blend until the fruit is finely chopped. Add the cream cheese and blend again. Transfer to a bowl and stir in the chocolate. Fold in the cream thoroughly.
2   Use about half this mixture to sandwich the biscuits together – it is easier if you do so in three stacks – and then press them together to create a log on a tray covered with baking parchment.
3   Use the remaining mixture to cover the log completely, making sure that no biscuits are visible. To finish the log-effect, use a fork to make a pattern that resembles tree bark. Chill overnight.
4   Just before serving, dust with icing sugar and arrange Christmas decorations on top.

These types of dessert will, I hope, be popular with many people. Whether you don't want to or simply cannot devote much time to preparing desserts or are put off by lengthy or involved recipes, these recipes are for you! I aim to demonstrate that desserts that are speedy to prepare can be as good as those that have taken a long time. It is important to use really good-quality 'cheat's' ingredients and to take trouble over presenting and decorating the dessert.

PUDDINGS IN A FLASH

You could make some of these puddings more special with a little extra something, for example, add kirsch to the raspberries in the Cheat's Raspberry Crème Brûlée (page 62) or brandy to Chocolate Fudge Fondue (page 64). Serve Chocolate Mint Ice Cream with Chocolate Mint Sauce (page 61) in chocolate cases, decorate with fresh mint leaves and surround the cases with a pool of the sauce.

This would be a **perfect dessert to serve after a Sunday lunch** — it could be put in the oven as you sit down to eat your roast. You could substitute pears or plums for the apples and vary the nuts accordingly.

APPLE, DATE & WALNUT PUDDING

125 g (4¹/₂ oz) self-raising flour
1 teaspoon ground cinnamon
1 teaspoon baking powder
100 g (3¹/₂ oz) caster sugar
45 ml (3 tablespoons) vegetable oil
45 ml (3 tablespoons) milk
3 medium eggs, separated
625 g (1 lb 6 oz) Bramley apples,
peeled, cored and cut into chunks
50 g (2 oz) dates, cut into small pieces
25 g (1 oz) walnut pieces

1 Preheat the oven to Gas Mark 5/electric oven 190°C/fan oven 170°C.
2 Sift the flour, cinnamon and baking powder into a bowl and stir in the caster sugar. Whisk the oil, milk and egg yolks together and pour over the flour mixture. Beat until smooth.
3 Whisk the egg whites until they are stiff.
4 Fold a spoonful into the mixture to loosen it and then gently fold in the remainder, followed by the apples, dates and walnuts.
5 Spoon into a greased 23 cm (9-inch) flan or gratin dish, level the surface and bake in the oven for about 40 minutes, until golden brown and firm to the touch (you may need to cover the top loosely with foil if it browns too quickly).
6 Serve warm, with custard or cream.

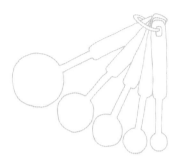

SERVES 6
PREPARATION TIME: 15 minutes + 30 minutes chilling
FREEZING: recommended

These little desserts are absolute heaven for all chocolate lovers and extremely easy to make. It is worth piping the mixture into the chocolate cases to create a professional finish.

CHOCOLATE MOUSSE CUPS

2 tablespoons dark chocolate spread (buy the best quality you can find)
150 ml (¼ pint) double cream, whipped
2 teaspoons instant coffee granules
15 ml (1 tablespoon) amaretto liqueur
6 amaretti biscuits
6 ready-made chocolate cases
toasted almonds or chocolate-coated coffee beans, to decorate

1 Soften the chocolate spread in a bowl and then fold in the whipped cream.
2 Dissolve the coffee in the amaretto liqueur and fold into the chocolate mixture.
3 Crumble an amaretti biscuit into the bottom of each chocolate case.
4 Spoon the chocolate mixture into a piping bag with a large star nozzle and pipe into the chocolate cases. Decorate with either the almonds or chocolate beans and chill for 30 minutes.

SERVES 4
PREPARATION TIME: 10 minutes
FREEZING: not recommended

This low-fat version of the famous dessert is quite delicious and incredibly easy to make. I think you would be surprised to know it hadn't been made with double cream. The addition of the raspberry coulis gives it an interesting dimension.

ETON MESS

250 g tub of ricotta cheese
150 g tub of Greek-style yoghurt
4 meringue nests, roughly crushed
225 g (8 oz) strawberries, hulled and
    quartered, plus extra to decorate
160 g jar of coulis de framboise

1 Place the ricotta cheese and yoghurt in a large bowl and mix thoroughly.
2 Fold in the crushed meringues and strawberries and divide between four glass dessert dishes.
3 Pour the raspberry coulis over the Eton Mess and decorate with some strawberries. Serve straight away.

SERVES 4
PREPARATION TIME:
15 minutes + 1 hour chilling
FREEZING: not recommended

This pudding is so quick and easy to prepare, mostly from storecupboard ingredients, but tastes as if you have spent a lot of time making it. For children, you could substitute orange juice for the rum.

SERVES 4–6
PREPARATION TIME: 20 minutes
FREEZING: recommended

Jamie Oliver inspired me to create this recipe.

I thought if he could create a recipe by combining Maltesers with ice cream then I could do one better, as this recipe has a sauce and only three ingredients are needed! This dessert is simplicity itself and will appeal to both adults and children alike.

RUM & RAISIN RICE PUDDING BRÛLÉE

CHOCOLATE MINT ICE CREAM WITH CHOCOLATE MINT SAUCE

80 g (3 oz) raisins
45–60 ml (3–4 tablespoons) rum
    or brandy
425 g can of creamed rice pudding
30 ml (2 tablespoons) crème fraîche
4 heaped teaspoons demerara sugar

1 Soak the raisins in the rum or brandy for at least 1 hour in a large bowl.
2 Preheat the grill. Add the rice pudding and crème fraîche to the raisins and combine well. Spoon into four ramekin dishes.
3 Sprinkle the demerara sugar evenly over the surface of the rice mixture and grill until the sugar has caramelised. Chill for an hour or until ready to serve.

1 litre (1³/₄ pints) good-quality
    vanilla ice cream
300 g box of After Dinner Mints
150 ml (¹/₄ pint) double cream

1 Place the ice cream in a bowl and allow to soften a little. Meanwhile, chop half the mints into small pieces. Fold the mint pieces into the ice cream, spoon into a freezer carton, cover and place in the freezer until you are ready to serve it.
2 To make the sauce, simply place the remaining mints and the cream in a saucepan over a gentle heat. When the mints begin to melt, stir until they have completely melted and the sauce has formed. It can either be served warm or cool.
3 To serve, simply scoop the ice cream into bowls and pour the sauce over.

SERVES 6
PREPARATION TIME: 20 minutes
FREEZING: recommended

SERVES 8
PREPARATION TIME: 15 minutes + 2 hours chilling
FREEZING: not recommended

CHOCOLATE & ORANGE TART

Jellies are generally quite sickly and synthetic but, using fresh orange juice and zest, you can create a dessert that tastes home-made and natural. If the pastry case you buy is not very deep, you may have too much filling; if this is the case, simply pour the surplus into wine glasses and you will have some chocolate mousses!

135 g packet of orange jelly
grated zest and juice of 2 large oranges, preferably Seville
100 g (3¹/₂ oz) plain chocolate
    (at least 70% cocoa solids), melted
150 ml (¹/₄ pint) double cream, whipped lightly
1 ready-made sweet pastry tart case
orange segments or grated chocolate, to decorate

1   Make the jelly with 200 ml (7 fl oz) of boiling water, adding the juice from the two oranges, which should yield about 100 ml (3¹/₂ fl oz). Allow to cool.
2   Whisk in the cooled, melted chocolate and orange zest. Fold in the whipped cream and pour into the pastry case. Place in the fridge to set for 1–2 hours.
3   Decorate with either orange segments or grated chocolate. Serve with cream.

CHEAT'S RASPBERRY CRÈME BRÛLÉE

This is quite delicious and tastes as if it has been made the traditional way. It takes just a few minutes to make. You could substitute any other soft fruit for the raspberries.

675 g (1¹/₂ lb) fresh raspberries
500 g tub of custard
250 g tub of mascarpone cheese
50 g (2 oz) caster sugar
200 g tub of crème fraîche
caster sugar, to glaze

1   Divide the raspberries between eight ramekin dishes.
2   Place the custard, mascarpone, sugar and crème fraîche in a large bowl and gently whisk until the mixture thickens. Then carefully spoon the mixture on to the raspberries and flatten the surface. Chill the mixture for at least 2 hours.
3   Sprinkle the surfaces generously with caster sugar and put under a hot grill to caramelise; serve straight away.

SERVES 6
PREPARATION & COOKING TIME: 25 minutes
FREEZING: not recommended

CINNAMON BRIOCHE TOAST WITH FRIED APPLES

Cinnamon toast is usually made with white bread; using brioche makes the dessert richer and sweeter and, I think, more interesting. Clotted cream or some really good-quality vanilla ice cream would be ideal accompaniments.

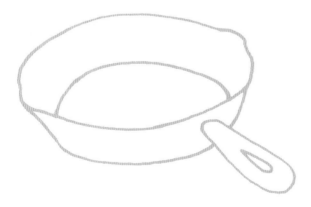

50 g (2 oz) sultanas
45 ml (3 tablespoons) brandy or apple juice
175 g (6 oz) unsalted butter
2 teaspoons ground cinnamon
6 slices of brioche
50 g (2 oz) light muscovado sugar
6 medium firm dessert apples,
  such as Cox's, peeled, cored and cut into 6–8 segments

1 Place the sultanas and brandy or apple juice in a bowl and leave to soak for 20 minutes. Preheat the oven to Gas Mark 2/electric oven 150°C/fan oven 130°C.

2 Heat half the butter in a large frying pan over a moderate heat, stir in the cinnamon and fry the bread, a couple of slices at a time, until golden brown and crisp. Place on a baking sheet, cover loosely with foil and keep warm in the oven.

3 Add the remaining butter to the frying pan, together with the sugar, and allow them to bubble together for a minute. Add the apple slices to the pan and increase the heat. Coat the apples in the buttery sugar and fry for a few minutes until the apples are golden brown and tender. Stir in the sultanas and the brandy or apple juice and heat through for a minute.

4 To serve, cut each slice of brioche toast in half diagonally and arrange on each serving plate, preferably warmed. Spoon over the apple slices and pan juices and serve with either clotted cream or ice cream.

CRÊPES GÂTEAU WITH BANOFFEE CREAM & BANANAS

pictured opposite

SERVES 6–8
PREPARATION TIME: 15 minutes
FREEZING: not recommended

**450 g jar of banoffee toffee sauce
(I used Merchant Gourmand's)
300 ml (½ pint) double cream,
whipped to soft peaks
4 ready-made crêpes
3 firm bananas, sliced
grated chocolate, to decorate**

I took this into my daughter's class for the children to taste and give their verdict. They thought it was **heavenly**, except for one who liked it except for the pancakes! It is very rich, but extremely easy to prepare, and both adults and children will love it. Most supermarkets stock ready-made pancakes/crêpes in their bakery departments.

1 Empty the banoffee toffee sauce into a bowl and fold in just over half the cream.
2 Place a crêpe on a serving plate, spread a third of the banoffee cream over it, evenly but not right to the edges, arrange a third of the banana slices on top, place another crêpe on top and repeat with the remaining cream and crêpes.
3 Spread the remaining whipped cream on to the fourth pancake before you place it on the gâteau. Sprinkle the grated chocolate on top of the cream and serve as soon as possible.

CHOCOLATE FUDGE FONDUE

SERVES 4–6
PREPARATION & COOKING TIME:
15 minutes
FREEZING: recommended

**150 ml (¼ pint) double cream
2 tablespoons dark chocolate spread
65 g Mars bar, cut into chunks
selection of fruit pieces,
such as bananas, grapes,
pears and strawberries, prepared
and cut up as necessary, to serve**

This decadent pudding will be popular with children and adults alike and is quick to make. You can kid yourself that **it's not that naughty** by serving it with lots of fruit!

1 Simply place the double cream, chocolate spread and Mars bar in a thick-bottomed saucepan and melt over a gentle heat, stirring from time to time, until all the ingredients have blended.
2 Arrange the fruit attractively on a large platter and place the fondue in a bowl in the centre. Using long forks, dip the fruit into the fondue.

NOTE: Alternatively, you could make the fondue in a fondue set, if you have one.

What can I say about chocolate and chocolate desserts? I just love them. I am passionate about chocolate and can never resist it. Much to the disgust of my family, I even have chocolate after breakfast. I simply cannot understand anyone who doesn't like chocolate!

In these recipes I have used all types of chocolate – white, plain/dark, milk and cocoa – and I have tried to create a wide variety of desserts: mousses, tarts, sauces, hot, cold and baked. Other chapters also include some chocolate recipes so there are plenty to choose from.

CHOCOLATE DESSERTS

Here are some tips for making chocolate puddings:

• Use the best quality chocolate you can, with the highest cocoa solids (at least 70%).

• Never use drinking chocolate instead of cocoa powder, because it is sweetened.

• When melting chocolate in a bowl over a pan of simmering water, make sure that no steam escapes from the pan, and that the water does not touch the bottom of the bowl, otherwise the chocolate will 'seize'. Should this happen, the situation can be saved by stirring in a little oil or butter. The slower the melting process, the better the end result.

• Never overheat melting chocolate, as the chocolate will lose its glossy appearance.

To avoid this happening, stir the chocolate as it melts and take it off the heat as soon as possible – quite often chocolate chunks hold their shape even when melted, until they are stirred.

• To accentuate chocolate flavour, dissolve some cocoa powder in a little hot water and stir into the mixture.

• White chocolate is not chocolate at all as it does not contain cocoa solids – it is a commercial product made from cocoa butter, milk and sugar. As with milk chocolate, it is sensitive to heat and so care needs to be taken when melting it.

Making chocolate curls or scrolls:

Melt 175 g (6 oz) of plain chocolate with 2 tablespoons of pure white vegetable fat, stirring until smooth. Pour into a small rectangular or square tin lined with foil or non-stick baking parchment to produce a block about 2.5 cm (1 inch) thick. Chill until set.

Allow the chocolate to come to room temperature, remove from the tin and use a swivel-bladed peeler to produce short, chunky curls.

To make longer curls or scrolls, pour the chocolate on to a marble slab or baking sheet and spread to a 3 mm (1/4 inch) thickness. When set, use the blade of a long, sharp knife at an angle of about 30° to scrape the chocolate into scrolls.

SERVES 4–6
PREPARATION TIME: 15 minutes
FREEZING: recommended

BITTER CHOCOLATE SAUCE

It is important to use good-quality chocolate with at least 70% cocoa solids for this recipe. It is so good that, if you're like me, you'll sneak a spoonful from the fridge when no one is looking. This sauce is delicious served with desserts such as ice cream, profiteroles, chocolate tart, poached pears and meringues.

3 tablespoons granulated sugar
175 g (6 oz) plain chocolate (at least 70%
cocoa solids), broken into pieces
25 g (1 oz) unsalted butter
75 ml (5 tablespoons) double cream

1 Place the sugar and 115 ml (4 fl oz) of water in a saucepan and bring to the boil, stirring from time to time until the sugar has dissolved.
2 Remove from the heat, add the chocolate and butter and stir until they have melted and the sauce is smooth. Finally, stir in the cream. The sauce can be served either warm or cold.

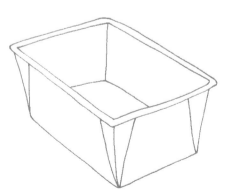

SERVES 6–8
PREPARATION TIME: 30 minutes + 2 hours chilling
FREEZING: recommended

CHOCOLATE HEAVEN

This is a dessert for all chocolate lovers. Please use the best chocolate you can buy – one that has at least 70% cocoa solids – as the end result will be far better.

If you live near an Italian delicatessen, try to buy Italian sponge fingers – they are delicious and perfect for this recipe.

110 g (4 oz) plain chocolate, broken into pieces
7.5 ml ('/₂ tablespoon) instant coffee granules
225 g (8 oz) cream cheese
15 ml (1 tablespoon) coffee liqueur, e.g. Tia Maria
1 tablespoon cocoa powder, sifted
150 ml ('/₄ pint) double cream, whipped
8 sponge fingers
about 150 ml ('/₄ pint) strong black coffee, cooled

1 Lightly oil a 450 g (1 lb) loaf tin and line with cling film.
2 Place the chocolate, coffee granules and 15 ml (1 tablespoon) of hot water in a bowl and place over a pan of hot water. Leave until the chocolate has melted, stirring from time to time. Cool slightly.
3 Fold into the cream cheese, with the liqueur and cocoa powder. Gently fold in the cream. Spoon half the mixture into the tin and level the surface.
4 Dip the sponge fingers into the coffee until they are soaked, being careful not to let them disintegrate, and arrange them side by side on top of the chocolate mixture. You may need to trim the ends of the sponge fingers a little.
5 Spoon on the remaining chocolate mixture, level the surface again and chill for 2 hours in the fridge to set.
6 To serve, unmould the terrine on to a plate, cut into slices, place on serving plates and surround with raspberry coulis.

SERVES 6
PREPARATION & COOKING TIME:
15 minutes + 25 minutes cooking + 2 hours chilling
FREEZING: not recommended

BOOZY CHOCOLATE CUSTARDS

These baked versions of chocolate mousse are a little bit like a baked chocolate cheesecake without the base. They are heavenly and I think they are better eaten a day or two after they have been made.

300 ml ('/₂ pint) double cream
150 ml ('/₄ pint) milk
115 g (4 oz) plain chocolate (at least 70% cocoa solids),
    broken into pieces
3 medium egg yolks
2 medium eggs
2 tablespoons demerara sugar
45 ml (3 tablespoons) dark rum or brandy

TO DECORATE:
whipped cream (see Note)
grated chocolate or chocolate curls,
    to decorate (see page 67)

1 Preheat the oven to Gas Mark 4/electric oven 180°C/fan oven 160°C.
2 Place the cream and milk in a saucepan and bring to the boil over a moderate heat. Remove from the heat, add the chocolate pieces and stir until the chocolate has melted.
3 Meanwhile, combine the egg yolks, eggs, demerara sugar and rum or brandy in a bowl and whisk gently to combine.
4 Pour the chocolate cream over the egg mixture, whisk to combine and then pass through a sieve. Lightly oil six ramekin dishes and pour the chocolate custard into the dishes.
5 Place the ramekin dishes in a roasting dish and pour boiling water into the roasting dish so that it is halfway up the sides of the ramekin dishes. Bake in the bottom of the oven, for 20-25 minutes until the custard is set and firm to a gentle touch.
6 Chill the custards, for 2 hours.
7 Put the whipped cream in a piping bag with a star nozzle. Decorate the mousses with cream rosettes and grated chocolate or chocolate curls.

NOTE: Whenever I have more cream than I need, I often pipe rosettes on to a tray, open-freeze them and then pop them into a bag. They are useful for instant decorations for desserts like this one.

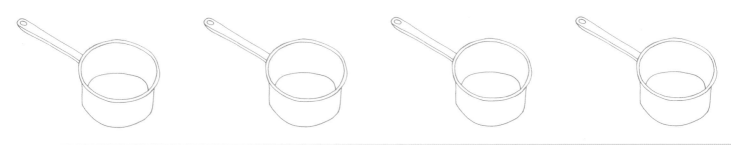

SERVES 8
PREPARATION TIME:
25 minutes + 2–3 hours chilling
FREEZING: recommended

This dessert **looks stunning** whether it is left whole or sliced on to dessert plates and surrounded by the coulis. The coulis complements the white chocolate beautifully, both in taste and appearance.

200 g (7 oz) good-quality white
chocolate, such as Lindt, broken
into pieces
11.7 g sachet of gelatine
500 g tub of Greek-style yoghurt
5 ml (1 teaspoon) vanilla extract
300 ml (¹/₂ pint) whipping cream,
whipped to soft peaks

FOR THE COULIS:
500 g (1 lb 2 oz) packet of frozen
summer fruit, thawed and drained
115 g (4 oz) caster sugar
45ml (3 tablespoons) kirsch
fresh mint leaves, to decorate

1 Melt the chocolate by placing it in a bowl over a pan of hot water and stirring occasionally until it has melted. Allow to cool.

2 Meanwhile, dissolve the gelatine by sprinkling it over 45 ml (3 tablespoons) of water, leaving it to go 'spongy' for a minute and then either placing in a bowl of hot water or in the microwave on full power for 30 seconds. Allow to cool.

3 Combine the yoghurt and vanilla extract in a large bowl and fold in the melted chocolate. Pour in the melted gelatine in a steady stream, while stirring. Finally, fold in the whipped cream and mix thoroughly. Spoon into a 900 g (2 lb) loaf tin that has been lightly oiled and lined with cling film. Chill for 2–3 hours, until set and firm.

4 Heat the summer fruits and sugar over a gentle heat until the sugar has dissolved and then pass the mixture through a nylon sieve into a bowl. Stir in the kirsch and then taste to ensure it is to the required sweetness.

5 Invert the terrine on to a serving platter, preferably oval in shape, decorate with the mint leaves and pour the coulis into a jug. If wished, you could slice the terrine on to the dessert plates and surround with the coulis.

WHITE CHOCOLATE TERRINE WITH SUMMER FRUIT COULIS

SERVES 6
PREPARATION & COOKING TIME:
30 minutes + 2 hours cooking
FREEZING: recommended

The addition of bananas to this steamed pudding makes it very light and moist. The white chocolate sauce, although rich, **complements it beautifully** both in taste and appearance – I would suggest you serve it in a flan dish so that the dish holds the sauce as you pour it over the top and it cascades down the sides.

DOUBLE CHOCOLATE & BANANA SPONGE PUDDING WITH WHITE CHOCOLATE SAUCE

175 g (6 oz) self-raising flour
25 g (1 oz) cocoa powder
80 g (3 oz) butter or margarine
2 large ripe bananas, mashed
80 g (3 oz) caster sugar
60 ml (4 tablespoons) milk
1 large egg
50 g (2 oz) plain chocolate,
broken into pieces

FOR THE SAUCE:
175 g (6 oz) white chocolate,
broken into pieces
150 ml (¼ pint) double cream

1　Half fill a large saucepan with water and bring it to the boil. Grease a 1-litre (1¾-pint) pudding basin thoroughly.

2　Sift the flour and cocoa together into a large bowl and rub in the butter or margarine until the mixture resembles breadcrumbs. Add the mashed bananas and sugar and stir into the mixture. Whisk the egg and milk together, add it to the sponge mixture and mix thoroughly. Finally, stir in the chocolate pieces.

3　Spoon the mixture into the basin and level the surface. Cover with foil (double thickness), making a pleat in the middle. Tie in place with string and make a string handle for lifting. Place in the saucepan and steam for 2 hours, topping up the water as necessary.

4　Just before the end of cooking time, place the white chocolate and cream in a bowl and place it over a saucepan of barely simmering water until the chocolate has melted into the cream. Remove it from the heat and stir it until it is smooth.

5　Run a knife around the sides of the pudding to loosen it and invert it on to a flan dish. Pour the white chocolate sauce over the top and serve.

SERVES 6
PREPARATION AND COOKING TIME:
40 minutes + 15 minutes chilling
FREEZING: recommended

I love Jaffa Cakes and thought it would be fun to create a sophisticated chocolate tart based on the same layers. The base is a shortbread one rather than the pastry normally associated with tarts as I think the texture is more suitable.

'JAFFA CAKE' TART

80 g (3 oz) plain flour
40 g (1½ oz) caster sugar
50 g (2 oz) butter, softened
115 g (4 oz) plain chocolate (at least 70% cocoa solids)
1 tablespoon butter, softened
30 ml (2 tablespoons) Cointreau
300 ml (½ pint) double cream, whipped
3 heaped tablespoons thin-cut orange marmalade
cocoa powder, to decorate

1 Preheat the oven to Gas Mark 6/ electric oven 200°C/fan oven 180°C.
2 Place the flour and sugar in a bowl and mix. Add the butter and rub into the flour mix. Bring the mixture together to form a ball, wrap in cling film and chill for 15 minutes.
3 Press the shortbread into the base of a 20 cm (8-inch) loose-bottomed flan tin, using a potato masher. Prick it lightly with a fork and bake in the oven for 10 minutes until golden brown. Allow to cool.

4 In the meantime, melt the chocolate with 30 ml (2 tablespoons) of water in a bowl set over a pan of barely simmering water. Remove from the heat and mix thoroughly. Stir in the tablespoon of butter followed by the Cointreau. Allow to cool for a few minutes and then fold in the whipped cream.
5 Spread the marmalade evenly over the shortbread base and then spoon over the chocolate mixture. Chill for at least 15 minutes to set, preferably overnight.
6 Sift some cocoa powder over the tart to decorate before serving.

SERVES 6
PREPARATION TIME: 10 minutes + 15 minutes cooking
FREEZING: not recommended for the pears
but recommended for the chocolate sauce

POACHED PEARS WITH CHOCOLATE SAUCE

I love this combination of delicately poached pears with a rich chocolate sauce. Both the pears and chocolate sauce can be prepared in advance and simply assembled before serving (the sauce will need to be re-heated gently).

6 ripe pears
30 ml (2 tablespoons) fresh lemon juice
80 g (3 oz) caster sugar
1 cinnamon stick

FOR THE SAUCE:
225 g (8 oz) plain chocolate (at least 70% cocoa solids)
50 g (2 oz) unsalted butter, cut into pieces
175 ml (6 fl oz) water
30 ml (2 tablespoons) brandy

1   Peel the pears, leaving the stalks intact. Scoop out the cores from the base and then brush the pears all over with lemon juice to prevent them from browning.
2   Place the sugar and 300 ml (½ pint) of water in a saucepan and heat gently until the sugar has dissolved. Add the pears and cinnamon stick, together with any remaining lemon juice and some more water if the pears are not completely covered. Bring to the boil, lower the heat, cover with a lid and simmer for about 15 minutes, until the pears are tender.
3   While the pears are cooking, make the chocolate sauce. Place the chocolate, butter and water in a saucepan and stir over a moderate heat until the chocolate and butter have melted. Whisk so that the sauce is smooth. Allow to cool a little and then stir in the brandy.
4   To serve, remove the pears with a slotted spoon from the syrup, transfer to the serving dish and keep warm. Boil the syrup over a high heat until it has reduced to 60 ml (4 tablespoons). Remove the cinnamon stick and stir it into the chocolate sauce. Pour the sauce over the pears and serve.

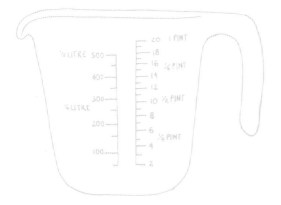

SERVES 4–6
PREPARATION & COOKING TIME:
25 minutes + 35–40 minutes cooking
FREEZING: not recommended

WHITE CHOCOLATE & VANILLA SOUFFLÉ

Most people shy away from making a hot soufflé as they think it's far too difficult. This recipe cheats a little by using ready-made custard. You can make most of the recipe (up to the egg whites) up to about an hour in advance. The recipe can be completed just before you sit down to your main course.

500 g carton of custard
1 vanilla pod
100 g bar of white chocolate, melted
4 large eggs, separated
150 ml (¹/₄ pint) double cream, whipped
sifted cocoa powder, to decorate

1 Preheat the oven to Gas Mark 6/electric oven 200°C/fan oven 180°C. Place a baking sheet in the oven. Brush melted butter generously on the inside of a soufflé dish that has a base with a diameter of 18 cm (7 inches) and is 9 cm (3¹/₂ inches high) don't worry if your dish is higher: the soufflé will rise just as well but won't rise above the dish. Dust the buttered surface with a little caster sugar.

2 Spoon the custard into a mixing bowl, split the vanilla pod lengthways and scrape the seeds into the custard. Pour in the melted white chocolate and stir to combine. Add the egg yolks, one at a time, stirring after each addition. Fold in the cream.

3 Whisk the egg whites in a large bowl until they are stiff. Fold a spoonful of the whites into the chocolate mixture using a large metal spoon, to loosen it, and then fold in the remainder using a figure-of-eight action. Quickly spoon the soufflé mixture into the prepared dish and run your little finger around the edge of the soufflé to help it rise well as it cooks.

4 Place the dish on the preheated tray and bake for 35–40 minutes – it should be well risen and there will be a little custard visible in the centre. Sprinkle with cocoa and serve immediately.

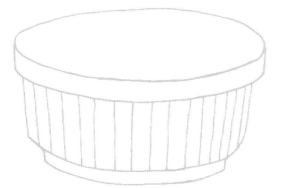

SERVES 6
PREPARATION TIME:
40 minutes + 35–40 minutes cooking
FREEZING: recommended

Most people drool when they are offered sticky toffee pudding. It's a **completely over-the-top pudding** but very satisfying. This version is very chocolatey and the butterscotch sauce complements it very well. You could serve it with crème fraîche, vanilla ice cream or even chocolate custard, if preferred.

115 g (4 oz) stoned dates, chopped
150 ml ('/₄ pint) water
'/₂ teaspoon bicarbonate of soda
1 heaped teaspoon instant coffee granules
50 g (2 oz) unsalted butter
115 g (4 oz) caster sugar
2 medium eggs, beaten
150 g (5 oz) self-raising flour
1 tablespoon cocoa powder
80 g (3 oz) plain chocolate, broken into small pieces
80 g (3 oz) walnut pieces

FOR THE SAUCE:
80 g (3 oz) dark muscovado sugar
80 g (3 oz) unsalted butter
150 ml ('/₄ pint) double cream

1 Put the dates in a saucepan with the water, bicarbonate of soda and coffee, bring to the boil and then leave to stand for 10 minutes.
2 Preheat the oven to Gas Mark 4/electric oven 180°C/fan oven 160°C. Place a roasting tin half filled with water in the oven. Grease and base-line six ramekins or teacups with discs of baking parchment or greased greaseproof paper.
3 Cream the butter with the sugar until light and fluffy, then gradually beat in the eggs. Sift the flour and cocoa together and fold into the mixture. Fold in the remaining ingredients, including the dates and their soaking liquid, mix well and divide between the ramekins or teacups. (It will look very wet at this stage.) Bake for 35–40 minutes until risen and firm to the touch – you may need to cover the tops with a sheet of foil towards the end of the cooking to prevent the tops from burning.
4 While they are cooking, make the butterscotch sauce. Place all the ingredients in a saucepan and stir until the sugar dissolves. Bring to the boil and boil for 2–3 minutes, stirring from time to time.
5 To serve, run a knife around the edges of the puddings and invert on to serving plates. Remove the parchment/greaseproof discs. Pour the sauce over the tops and serve straight away.

STICKY MOCHA PUDDINGS WITH BUTTERSCOTCH SAUCE